The Struggle For Economic Support Of The Indigenous Business Women In Zimbabwe

The Struggle For Economic Support Of The Indigenous Business Women In Zimbabwe

Lindiwe Chopamba

Doctor Of Business Administration

To order additional copies of this book, contact:
Xlibris Corporation
1-888-795-4274
www.Xlibris.com
Orders@Xlibris.com
73663

Table of Contents

Chapter

Chapter 1

Introduction

Historical Background of an African Woman

From birth, an African woman is regarded as a simple, humble creature that is to marry away from home. She is a symbol of child rearing and the material world. Her male counterpart is honored and respected as one to inherit the father's land. Due to assigned roles for males and females, certain privileges are allotted only to the male. These include the opportunity of going to school and outside employment. The virtues of spiritual inheritance are generally denied to women. (1)

Certain cultures also do not allow women to hold hierarchical instruments of authority. Thus, this spiritual endowment makes woman appear inferior as they are deprived of certain cultural and economic privileges. Nevertheless, whatever might be their cultural deprivation, women are entrusted with caring for the family morals and the children's daily needs. The male traditionally protects and guides the household's spiritual and long-term material needs.

Since the colonial days, many women in Africa have aspired to and reached positions of prominence. They belong to different societies of the market women. (2)

In Zimbabwe, women fought hand in hand with their male counterparts against colonialism. They were formidable in their fights and agitations because they had a common enemy.

The resistance to Portuguese colonial rule in Angola, Mozambique, and Guinea-Bissau encouraged the greater mobility of women involved in the movement. (Rich, 1975)

In 1929 women organized against the colonial rule in Southern Nigeria. The Southern Nigerians fought the administrative officers when they introduced a tax system on women, and this policy was vehemently challenged by all women's organizations. About thirty-two women were shot and killed. About thirty of them were wounded. The mishandling of women's resistance in 1929 revealed the weakness of the colonial administration in Africa. From that day on, all women on the African Continent have increased their search for liberation and identity.

The social and economic roles played by African women, particularly by the market women, need closer investigation.(3) Such investigation will help to change their long history of low position and second-class status.

The whole problem of African women's education on cultural traditions allowed only the male to go to school. The disfavor customarily began at birth, when arrival of a female child brought disappointment or dishonor to the families in societies that placed a premium on male children.

With the advent of the missionaries, education was open only to male children. The townspeople did not want to have their girls educated. Their philosophy was that book knowledge was power and that power should be retained in the hands of men.

The early twentieth century was a period of transformation in Africa. Schools were opened to woman. For the first time females began to compete with their male counterparts for certain governmental jobs. Despite this, women's education is still mainly in domestic science, cooking needlework housekeeping and laundry, but the courses were planned to give them morals and discipline in accordance with African culture and traditions. The influence of the Christian churches was felt tremendously in the education of African women.

The missionary Societies and the Roman Catholic churches competed very strongly for the education of the women in Africa.

The basic curriculum in the school included Bible stories, prayers, music, arithmetic, geography, and English. Simple English was taught, as this was then thought to be the language of commerce and civilization.

One of the major signs of Christianity's influence on women in Africa was the replacement of polygamy with monogamy.

In certain areas the church built convents where girls, especially those intending to get married in the church, were kept. They attended marriage encounter courses and were introduced to the philosophy of one man / one wife. At times forces were used to gather girls together who were preparing for marriage to stay in the convent until they got married in the church. This approach was carried out more forcefully by the Roman Catholic Church.

With the increase of women's education in different fields of learning, the subordinate position of woman is now being challenged. Custom permitted African men to have more than one wife, provided the rituals of obtaining them were met. Such ideas of plural marriage are no longer being accepted with good grace.

Women's acceptance of the African man as "god of all creations" in his house does not necessarily mean that women have no rights of their own. Whatever the men might think of the women's positions they nevertheless indirectly govern their respective households.

Our grandmother had women's liberation long before it became popular in the West.

Women, though considered weak, could not tolerate a few abuses from the education of woman in the initial period of the arrival of the missionaries which was the pillars of the missionaries evangelization and education. They wanted their children, particularly males, to learn the white man's education.

Woman's morals and their sense of duty reflect their positions within the societies. They continue to attend to their families' needs, thereby confirming the importance of women in the family.

Twentieth century African woman have abandoned a few ideas of their culture, but the characteristics of the market women have not changed. These women, bound by their traditional and customary laws, concern themselves only with domestic work.

Colonial governments were resignedly implemented by men. Men's cowardly acts might be attributed on part to fears of being victimized by the colonial overlords and their African representatives. Unlike African men, early Europeans who came to Africa accorded a certain respect to woman. Often they avoided having conflicts with women's market associations which were and still are the strongest organizations in Africa.

European colonialists often regarded African men as subhuman and forced them to accept their orders at gun point. In order to implement the direct rule of African people, the powers of the warrant chiefs, police, and court messengers were strengthened. Men would dash into the bushes for safety whenever the policemen or court messengers visited the village, while the women would stay behind to protest any government proposals that were contrary to their way of life. They would demonstrate through their organizations while their husbands were in the bush avoiding arrest.

The hostile attitudes of such colonial administrators were not acceptable to African women. They demonstrated against the government in protest of imposition of any laws. At times they met with violence while forcing their wishes through.

The organizations are now more oriented to economic development than pre-independence political consciousness. Because of the economic power held by some of these market women, the Western world has recognized their importance. African women's main problems seem to differ little from those of women from the Western world; however, their problems are more concerned with economic freedom and the "good life." In these areas they are far behind their Western counterparts.

Women in the rural areas are subjected to the worst disabilities such as illiteracy, poverty, starvation, scarcity of water, lack of medical care, and many other obstacles at stake.

Background Of Zimbabwe Women

The struggle for the liberation of Zimbabwe has a long history stretching back to the last century when large numbers of white people entered the country and occupied the land. Many women and girls took part in the final war of independence that led to majority rule in 1980. They could draw inspiration form the fact that one of the major leaders of the first resistance to white rule was a woman, Nehanda. Today the women of Zimbabwe have won their fight but in the last century, Nehanda was to suffer and die for her courage.

There is a tradition that the original Nehanda lived sometime in the fifteenth century and was the daughter of a chief of the northern Shona. Although the original Nehanda disappeared, her sprit returns as a guardian of her people. The Shona, for their part would never forget the courage of Nehanda and the tradition of a Nehanda medium continued. Many years later, in 1972, an old lady in her mid-eighties who was possessed by the Nehanda spirit, was taken form her home to a safe place on Zambezi river by ZANLA guerrillas fighting against the white Rhodesians. The guerrillas consulted her about where to hide arms, what routes to take and where to fight. They called the northern area of fighting the Nehanda Sector. This medium died on June 12, 1973. One day her remains will be taken back to her home in Zimbabwe for burial. Who can deny that at last Nehanda had her victory? (4)

The liberation of the women of Zimbabwe was a fundamental necessity of the revolution, the guarantee of its continuity, and the precondition for its victory. The main objective of Chimurenga (revolutionary war) was to destroy the system of exploitation and to build a new society which releases the potentialities of human beings. In their active participation in the liberation of Zimbabwe, the women made it very clear about the objectives of the struggle. They fought for national independence and sexual equality. To them, the two things are inseparable and they insist that to simply fight for improved status within the framework of a racist, oppressive system, is quite meaningless. The achievement of independence to them is the best guarantee for changing the situation they are in and for guaranteeing the establishment of equal rights for all, irrespective of race, color, or sex. The Universal Declaration of Human Rights states that everyone has the right to take part in the government of his or her country. The empowerment and autonomy of women, and the improvement of women's social, economic and political status, is essential for the achievement of both transparent and accountable government and administration, and sustainable development in all areas of life. The power relations that prevent women form leading fulfilling lives operate at many levels of society, from the most personal to the highly public.

Achieving the good of equal participation of women and men in decision making will provide a balance that more accurately reflects the composition of society and is needed in order to strengthen democracy and promote its proper functioning. Equality in political decision making performs a leverage function without which it is highly unlikely that a real integration of the equality dimension in government policy making is feasible.

In this respect, women's equal participation in political life plays a pivotal role in the general process of the advancement of women. Women's equal participation in decision making is not only a demand for women's interests to be taken into account.

Without the active participation of women in the incorporation of women's perspective at all levels of decision making, the goals of equality, development, and peace cannot be achieved.

Despite the widespread movement towards democratization in most countries, women in Zimbabwe are largely under represented at most levels of government, especially in ministerial and executive bodies, and have made little progress in attaining political power in legislative bodies or in achieving the target endorsed by the Economic and Social Council of having 30 percent women in positions at decision making levels. Globally, only 10 percent of the members of legislative bodies and a lower percentage of ministerial positions are now held by women. Indeed, some countries, including those that are undergoing fundamental political, economic, and social changes have seen a significant decrease in the number of women represented in legislative bodies. Although women make up at least half of the electorate in Zimbabwe, and have attained the right to vote, they continue to be seriously under-represented as candidates for public office.

The traditional working patterns of many political parties and government structures continue to be barriers to women's participation in public life. Women in Zimbabwe are discouraged form seeking political office by discriminatory attitudes and practices, family and child care responsibilities, and the high cost of seeking and holding public office. Women in politics and decision making positions in governments and legislative bodies contribute to redefining political priorities, placing new items on the political agenda that reflect and address women's gender specific concerns, values, and experiences, providing new perspectives on mainstream political issues.

Zimbabwean woman have demonstrated considerable leadership in community and informal organizations, as well as in public office. However, socialization and negative stereotyping of woman and men, including stereotyping through the media, reinforces the tendency for political decision making to remain the domain of men. Likewise, the under-representation of women in decision making positions in the areas of art, culture, sports, the media, education, religion, and the law have prevented women form having a significant impact on many key institutions.

Owing to their limited access to the traditional avenues to power, such as the decision making bodies of political parties, employer organizations and trade unions, Zimbabwean women have gained access to power through alternative structures, particularly in the non-governmental organization sector. Through non-governmental organizations and grass roots organizations, women have been able to articulate their interest and concerns, and have placed women's issues on the national, regional, and international agendas.

Inequality in the public arena is often started with discriminatory attitudes and practices and unequal power relations between women and men within the family. The unequal division of labor and responsibilities within households, based on unequal power relations, also limits women's potential to find time to develop the skills required for participation in decision making in wider public forums. A more equal sharing of those responsibilities between women and men not only provides a better quality of life for women and their daughters, but also enhances their opportunities to shape and design public policy, to shape and design practice and expenditure so that their interests may be recognized and addressed. Informal networks and patterns of decision making at the local community level that reflect a dominant male ethos, restrict women's ability to participate equally in political, economic, and social life.

The low proportion of women among economic and political decision makers at the local, national, and regional levels reflects structural and attitudinal barriers that need to be addressed through positive measures. Government, national corporations, the mass media, banks, academic and scientific institutions and international organizations do not make full use of women's talents as top level managers, policy makers, diplomats, and negotiators.

The equitable distribution of power and decision making at all levels is dependent on the government and other actors undertaking statistical gender analysis and mainstreaming a gender perspective in both policy development and the implementation of programs. Equality in decision making is essential to the empowerment of women. National, regional, and international statistical institutions still have insufficient knowledge of how to present the issues related to the equal treatment of women and men in the economic and social spheres.

In particular, there is insufficient use of existing data bases and methodologies in the important sphere of decision making.

In addressing the inequity between men and women in the sharing of power and decision making at all levels, the government of Zimbabwe and other actors should promote an active and visible policy of mainstreaming a gender perspective on all policies and programs so that before decisions are made, an analysis is taken of the effects on women and men, respectively.

References

1. Nijoku, John E. Everegula *The World of the African Woman* copyright 1980 by John E. Nijoku in United States of America
2. Christine Obbo, *African Women, Their Struggle for Economic Independence* Zed Press, 57 Caledonian Road, London. 1980
3. The world of African Women.
4. African Historical Biographies, Women Leaders in African History, Sweetman, David 1943. Chapter 12, page 97

Further Reading

The Woman and International development, Annual Volume 1 & 2 Edited by Rita S. Callin, Marilyn Arnoff, and Anne Fergusson.

David Martin and Phyllis Johnson: The Struggle for Zimbabwe. (London: Faber, 1981: Harare: Zimbabwe Published House 1982)

Chapter 2

Women and Education

Education is an important determinant of the nature of and rewards to women's work, both in the market and in the home. Women's probability of being in the labor force, continuity of participation over the life cycle, earnings, occupational attainment, fertility and allocation of time across household tasks all vary with educational attainment. Highly educated women have been offered employment opportunities in the growing white collar occupations and have been able to take advantage of the breakdown in occupational segregation in the professions since the 1970's. A society can be measured as many have said, by the manner in which it nurtures and treats its children.

Education, the acquisition of knowledge, is the key ingredient for developing and nurturing children, young adults, and society at large. When you know better, you do better. Education is paramount for the survival and success of all Zimbabweans and other women in the Third World. Education's ultimate goal should be training students so they can live full lives, adapt to change, and attribute to productive work and service to others.

In order to promote real equality of opportunity, education policy should aim not only to provide equal access in formal terms, for boys and girls, or men and women, in all stages and sectors of the education system, but also, without doubt, to achieve practical equality for access to equally valuable educational provision. (1)

It is thus critical to focus upon instances and areas where inequalities between the sexes in education and training remains outstanding and upon the barriers and impediments that frustrate more equal chances. Many studies have demonstrated the enduring nature of female educational disadvantage. (2) Despite progress in overall participation levels, significant differences remain and a continuing division between the sexes is still clear in terms of subjects studied, particularly in vocational education and training. The removal of formal barriers of access to girls and woman is by no means tantamount to realizing actual equality of educational opportunity and results.

In this chapter the author examines the position of girls and women in education systems. For this reason, it excludes discussion of in-firm training and management training areas that are critical for women. This will be discussed in the next chapters.

This chapter seeks to describe the patterns of inequalities between the sexes in education rather than analyze and explain them, which would require much more extensive treatment and would have to take account of differences in national systems.

Across the world, significant improvements have been made in women's education, health, and access to labor market opportunities. However, compared with men, women remain at a socio-economic disadvantage.

Both boys and girls have benefited from enormous expansion in school enrolments at all levels of education in Zimbabwe, but girls still lag behind.

In developing countries in 1960, there were 67 females per 100 males enrolled in primary school. In 1990, there were 86 females per 100 males enrolled. Trends are similar for secondary and tertiary enrolments, with 53 females per 100 males.

Most governments have acted to remove formal barriers to entry into school systems and give access to girls and boys. Laws regarding compulsory attendance are widespread.

According to United Nations' records, 161 of 194 countries with autonomous school systems had compulsory schooling by 1980. Of these, most countries, 94 of the 161, required eight to ten years of schooling. Fifty-five required seven years or less. Fewer than twelve required ten years or more.(3)

A remarkable rise in school enrolment over the post-war period therefore gives ground for optimism that education has become a major force for the improvement of women's lives and status. Statistics, which are more abundant on this subject than on employment, (4) can tell us how far girls' education has advanced over these years. The increases in numbers enrolled in school are substantial.

It is evident that large disparities still exist, however, and the record is not complete without a look at these deficiencies as a guide to the progress which must still be made.

Despite these favorable trends, it is also apparent that basic elementary education is not yet available to a large proportion of the world's children and that girls are particularly disadvantaged. Laws requiring compulsory education are not uniformly enforced. Equality of education for women suffers not only from a lack of access to schooling, but also from the restrictive stereotypes outside of school and in the education process itself. A stereotype of what is natural and acceptable for each sex creates subtle barriers to the full development of intellectual abilities even when academics are unlimited.

In Zimbabwe culture, the socialization process begins at the earliest ages within the family and community. Culturally imposed sex roles and constraints shape self images, attitudes, and ambitions. The process is common to all societies, although much more rigidly observed in some. In general, girls are expected to be passive and obedient, boys active, competitive, and combative.

Even modern media of communication tend to reinforce sex stereotypes, e.g. advertising consistently identifies women with household cleaning products and men with machinery and advanced technology.

Conclusions and Policy Directions

The factors that lie behind these patterns of inequality are manifold and complex. Several studies place emphasis upon the potential of the school, and teachers in particular, to change attitudes held by girls and boys towards school subjects and attainment with the aim of encouraging girls into a broader range of fields. But it is clear that any changes in attitudes and aspirations that schools might foster could only have an impact as part of a coherent set of policies to widen labor market opportunities for women, as shall be discussed through this paper.

Education does, however, have a significant responsibility and role to play and there are many features of policy and the organization of learning that do affect the patterns of segregation. Recognition of this has led several countries to establish special commissions with responsibility for reducing sex inequalities in education and, in certain cases to adopt general legislation prohibiting discrimination by sex in educational practices. It is commonly recognized, however, that most of the problems reside in informal practices, organization structures and widespread influences rather than formal discriminatory arrangements. A number of the more important areas through which educational change can contribute to greater equality between the sexes can be identified.

One major area is the organization of education itself, particularly the nature and timing of specialization into branches and tracks with a preponderance of one sex. The timing and nature of specialization is of great importance to the educational careers of girls and boys. In countries where specialization begins early in the school career, the patterns which are apparent later in education and training prove difficult to change, having been institutionalized at an early juncture. Time tabling practices can also narrow the options open to girls because certain school subjects are sometimes only available when taken in combination with others with which they are conveniently associated. Whether they leave school early or continue to pursue their studies to a more advanced level, girls who have specialized early in over subscribed subjects may in fact find themselves caught in an educational process which in many cases leads to unemployment.

The role of teachers is of course a vital one in helping pupils to make informal decisions concerning school subjects and training fields. This is true both generally, throughout education and more specifically in the guidance and counseling that is offered or, perhaps equally pertinently not offered.

It is a factor that should receive much more attention in the initial training for teachers, and in in-service training, particularly because the processes whereby sex, typed images, and learning, are reinforced are so implicit and hidden, yet pervasive.

Teachers and staff themselves provide very concrete models along sex-typed lines. Relatively few school or college directors are female. Male science and female arts teachers and, to even greater extent, female primary and pre-primary staff are the norm. Staff recruitment and teacher training policies could take account of this more explicitly. Some countries have already introduced measures with the aim of encouraging more men into pre-primary and primary teacher training. At the same time, efforts should be made to allow women to enter non-traditional teaching fields and positions of authority. These considerations apply to all levels of education and training, general or vocational, and not just to mainstream primary an secondary schooling.

Young women at he end of their schooling face a serious lack of opportunity, with a severely limited range of training options open to them, limited in terms of occupational fields, and in terms of places on extensive training courses. This problem is raised, if anything, even more sharply for older women. Training that would enable promotion or a realignment of careers, organized by or through the work place, is generally much more restricted for women than men. There is also a pressing need for suitable learning places for those who wish to re-enter the paid labor market after a number of years absence, a problem that has not been treated in this chapter, which has confined itself to school education.

The data the author has presented in this chapter leads to the general conclusion that, at the school level, the problem is no longer one of female under-participation in post compulsory education, as measured in years of schooling, although under-participation persists at the level of higher education in many countries. Rather, the problem concerns the type of education that girls receive. They are leaving school with a limited range of employment options, increasingly confined to areas in which competition for available jobs is increasing.

References

1. The Integration of Women into the Economy 1985 p.121
2. Q.E.C.D. 1985 p. 121
3. Women, a World Survey, by Ruth Leger Sivard 1985 chapter 18.
4. Women, a World Survey, by Ruth Leger Sivard 1985 chapter 18.

Chapter 3

Market Women in Zimbabwe
Rural Development

The experience of Zimbabwean women in their struggle of economic development is similar to those of other women moving through social, political, and economic changes. The struggle to overcome obstacles that have created barriers to their economic and social emancipation is often in conflict with their traditional culture.

The most pressing problem for Zimbabwean women, besides the education of their children, is the increase of their subsistence production of agriculture, which in turn will increase their industrial production. When the income of the rural population increases, it will limit the number of women who plan to migrate to the urban areas for a better living. As women's work at home is never ending, so also is the role of women in the rural economies remains unfulfilled.

For most women on the rural farms of Zimbabwe, the great opportunity is still a dream. Women have often desired some technical training, but they are often neglected by the extension officers. The input and output of the rural Zimbabwean women is an indication that they need more and better training in agricultural production and marketing for them to achieve good and profitable marketing, better policies and programs should be pursued for the benefit of the rural women farmers.

In Zimbabwe, individual participation has been common among women themselves, but more co-operative participation is necessary in development activities, as procedures and policies of implementing the idea of new farm settlement and development do not yet appear to be clearly understood.

The policy makers should make a long-range plan that will fit into a new situation and improve the workers' social conditions. This program will focus on building a more satisfying and rewarding way of life for the women of Zimbabwe and their families.

The farm women believe that agriculture should have an equality of income with the non-agricultural sector of the economy. Obviously they are aware of the substantial concentration of economic power in the non-farm economy, which is often wielded to the disadvantage of the rural families. A common sign of decline in agricultural prices and income can be seen in the outcries of the producers of commodities and also by the market women.

The pressing issues are how to increase per-capita output and how the commodities produced on the farms may move more rapidly from the rural areas to the consumers.

The women farmers are ignorant of what happens along the marketing chain. While the marketing boards fix the prices by law for the consumer and producer, there is no attempt on the part of most of the marketing boards to include market women in planning and agricultural policies.

National policy is not made in such a way as to protect the women and other users of farm products. The problems of the rural planning are difficult enough, yet the government will do such disservice to its nation if it carelessly permits emotions to blind it to the need for a more careful analyses of how best to bring every relevant bit of knowledge to its improvement.

In fact, the development of agriculture and markets should be the primary concern for all African governments. The problem of expanding and improving product per acre is most vital because it concerns the largest section of the population and the most important sector of the African economy.

Zimbabwean women are thirsty for the fruits of human labor that already exist in the developed world. The Zimbabwean women will certainly reject an ideology that does not place in women a true disposition for the things of this earth or that alienates them in any way from the pursuit of technological improvements of the material world. At the same time, they yearn to preserve the values integral to their personal worth and integrity. They have long experienced the dehumanization of their person and the devaluation of their worth by different cultures. The refusal of males to consider them equal in the same family has intensified their struggle for liberation. The elite among them refuse to accept unequal partnership.

There are many difficult problems to be tackled besides ignorance and bad methods of production. Besides implements created by the land tenure, social and religious conventions, habits, traditional attitudes toward the land and manual work, one crop cultivation and low productivity, financial assistance is urgently needed.

The position of women will not be improved if new techniques are transferred piecemeal, but every transfer of a new technique implies change in several dimensions.

All the women throughout Zimbabwe have shown a considerable response to economic incentives that will increase production. However, agricultural innovations that reduce technical risks have not gained a precise and scientific understanding among the women.

It is hoped that the co-operative movements introduced into women's organizations can play a substantial part in encouraging savings in good years and granting credit in bad ones. Co-operative marketing may be encouraged by government aids and subsidies in order to be able to store the members' commodities. There is a great need for technical skills.

Zimbabwean women are looking for technical and economic progress in farming and farm products. They are in great need of technical progress that arises from the new knowledge of the soil animal diseases, pests, and implements a tool. Economic progress in agriculture has required more than technical knowledge alone. Directing extension services to the rural family will guarantee many new benefits to Zimbabwean women.

Malnutrition, transportation problems, bad housing and sanitation, and diseases are some of the obstacles to rural development in Zimbabwe. Improvement in these areas is now long overdue. Development of credit programs, introduction of small tractors and plows, made to fit well into peasant agriculture will have much impact if made available to the rural farm woman of Zimbabwe.

The continued neglect of woman in rural development by the extension specialists all over Zimbabwe seems to show that there is a bias for future growth of a sound Zimbabwean economy. (1) The major aim of the extension people should be to stress the importance of domestic production of agricultural consumer goods for the expansion of local markets.

As a result of the attitudes of the extension service, the gap between the labour productivity of men and women thus continues to widen. Men are taught to apply modern methods in the cultivation of a given crop, while women continue to use traditional methods in the cultivation of a given crop, thus getting less output form their efforts than men. The inevitable result is that women are discouraged from participating in agricultural development and are glad to abandon cultivation whenever their husband's income makes it possible.

Women in African culture are mostly responsible for food production, and this suggests that the entire responsibility of agricultural production rested mostly with women who turn the soil, sowed, weeded, and harvested. Despite the fact that disguised unemployment lingers around the rural farm, there are fluctuations in yield, especially during the period of harvest, when the commodities harvested reach the market at the same time.

In the markets, some basic commodities are very high during the producing seasons, and after the season. The main reasons for this are:

a. The production per acre is very low.
b. The scarcity of such home crops in the market.
c. Sharp fluctuations in export crops may affect the producer's prices.
d. Crop failures during a series of bad seasons.

All over Africa historical conferences on women have emphasized that there is no national development plan inimical to women. (2) It has recently become an axiom that women are the main source of production and marketing of foods in Africa. But the question remains whether women's food production ever kept pace with African population so as to produce enough food for the export market. What women often discuss in their organizations is how the economy can provide the increasing population with a modern standard of living. The problem of supplying adequate food and well-balanced meals presents a definite challenge to woman and children.

The marketing margin between the producers and the world market is so large that as a result, the women producers usually receive a lower price for their crops than do men. It is certain that the rural farmers are not expecting the prices that are prevailing in the world market, nor are they seeking to equalize the substantial concentration of economic power in the non-farm economy, which is often wielded to the disadvantage of women.

Zimbabwean women have clearly understood the loss of potential in their role in rural development for decades. To breach the gaps that have existed between men and women, the most pressing need now is to increase production and thereby receive a fair price to enable women to meet their national and international commitments. It has been substantially proven that, despite all claims, women are keys to agricultural production and distribution for domestic consumption. Inadequate food programs are no longer rated as news. To increase per-capita income on the rural farm the agricultural planners should reinforce the popular statements from the non-farm groups, who often have the feeling that it is necessary to have agricultural prosperity in order to maintain national economic prosperity.

Zimbabwean women have no land rights, just as well as all African women. (3) Their culture does not allow them to dispose of any piece of land, although they could use the land for the production of food, by the virtue of being a wife, sister, daughter, or cousin.

Surely women's lack of land ownership brings insecurity and uncertainty in the production of agriculture and availability of food. Could such land tenure be changed to favour the women?

The statutory land rights in many African countries do not favor women, while at the same time they agree with the customary laws in letting the male dispose of the land. (4) In most African countries land tenure can only be accurately spoken of as "communal" or tribal. Tenure can be said to be communal when the "commune" (that is, the land-holding unit) is concerned as a social unit whose membership confers certain rights in land upon the individual and in which the individual cultivator exercises all acts of ownership except that of alienation. Both the individual and the group enjoy certain well-defined rights in the use of land. The rural people regard land as a social unit, such as the clan, tribe, village, and extended family. The land is the responsibility of the head of the family who is the caretaker. The family is the real owner of land, but an operator can use the land and dispose of his crop in the interest of the community.

The term "community" may refer to a family, a clan, kindred or lineage group. In most of rural African areas, the land belongs to many, the living, the dead, and countless numbers unborn. Land is and heirloom of the family, the kinship, and the extended family. The sanction of customary tenure against the sale of misuse of land arises from the universal belief that the land is a sacred trust held by the present generation of users on behalf of the dead ancestors of the group as well as unborn generations.

Individuals are prohibited from disposing of land of the group either by sale or mortgage. Land is not a negotiable property, and is as such not heritable and alienable by individuals. In Africa the condition of land tenure is practically the same except for a few small differences from country to country. With all these arrangements, women are completely excluded from tenure arrangements. The use of land was transferable and inherited, but the evidence was overwhelming that this power remains with the male, while the female who mainly operates the land continues to be a tenant. (5)

Zimbabwean land arrangements are the continuity of different customary laws inherited by traditions. If the present economies of this country continue to pursue this development pattern, the positions of women will remain substantially unchanged. Males register the land in their names to the disadvantage of the females who use the land for food production.

In consideration of the rural development, women's organizations everywhere are questioning the roles that have been assigned to them and the values on which the roles are based. Land ownership by traditional arrangement has not been favorable to African women, but the women through their organizations are drawing strength to face the challenge. (6)

The customs have assigned the males to inherit the land in African societies, but could this subjugation code of tradition be tempered so that women could share the land rights, the women asked? All over the globe women are coming out to speak for themselves. (7) They boldly speak in two camps, namely the traditional women and the liberated women. Zimbabwean women surely fall into the first camp, as their standard of living is low.

Most women desire some form of education, either from their government or United Nations organizations, on how to produce more food for the growing population.

The Savings Movement among Rural Market Women of Zimbabwe

The savings movement is rapidly gaining ground among rural women in Zimbabwe. Savings clubs are being formed by the hundreds. Entirely autonomous organizations, the clubs are composed of like-minded women from the same area who contribute to a collective savings fund on which they can draw to purchase farm inputs and implements or to pay school fees, health costs, and other social expenses. First launched by a Christian organization as a combination of traditional credit societies and formal credit unions, the savings clubs movement got fully under way after independence.

It now has more than 200,000 members in over 5,700 clubs; 97 percent are women, most of them farmers. Traditionally, women have had no access to institutional credit since the marketing of surplus crops on which such access depends is done mostly by men. The average size of a club is about 35 members; each elects a chairman and treasurer who are jointly responsible for keeping the accounts. Most clubs meet once a week and the members are encouraged to make small deposits regularly. The meetings provide an opportunity not only for discussing savings but also exchanging information and experience and hence serve to strengthen solidarity among the members. The women gain self confidence and economic independence since their savings constitute capital over which they exercise full control.

In addition, the clubs are able to secure assistance from local extension services in familiarizing the women with new technology and agricultural techniques, and in purchasing supplies wholesale.

As their capital increases, some clubs engage in collective ventures such as poultry and vegetable farming for the market. The clubs also receive technical guidance from the Savings Development Movement, a non-governmental organization established to provide them with training facilities, assistance in auditing their accounts and general operational flexibility. Their ability to initiate reforms, however, is limited by their informal status. They have not yet obtained assistance from the banking system, which remains inaccessible to the movement, or been able to establish a savings bank especially designed to meet the needs of the rural poor.

Summary

The issue is no longer whether Zimbabwean women's aim and roles are realized in the world of men, but what types of roles are still unfulfilled? Women need programs that will stress their important roles in rural development. Such programs will attack the symptoms of their problems and also the basic causes that reduce the regional inequalities in per capita income. The author stressed at length that women have not been fully favored in rural development.

In this discussion the author may look into some economic facts regarding rural development and women. There are four facts that planners, policy makers, and researchers should consider in Zimbabwe rural-development plans:

1. The demand for agricultural development products is inelastic. This is true for all cash crop products such as cotton, groundnuts and maize. This means that the women producers get less when the supply of each of these commodities is increased. In short, it means that from most agricultural commodities, the total gross income returned to the producers is smaller for a large crop than for smaller

crops. This does not insure equitable redistribution of income dislocated by their economic situations. Though it is perhaps not always recognized, it is certainly true that any change which would produce better conditions for women themselves showed awareness and expressed a positive desire for such change aggressively.

The development of agriculture is essential for the home market and other economic activities. When the income is derived from agriculture and the country's activities grow, the internal market for consumer goods grows automatically, thus enhancing the promotion of small industries. One of the aims of rural development is to increase food production so as to meet the needs of an expanding population. The women, the model for peace, have openly expressed through their societies that the way to promote progress in the world is to increase the production of food. (8)

In underdeveloped countries agriculture and industries are complementary and not competitive. In this era, if planners and economists in Zimbabwe want to proceed with industrialization without improving the agricultural sector of the economy, it will ruin the agricultural sector. Failure to improve women in agriculture is to ruin the aim of rural development. Low productivity may be complicated, because socio-economic structures may contribute to the women's failure.

2. The main problem of rural development is that many women in agricultural economies are very unproductive and as a result they have little or no income. This may be due to the level of technique upon the capital or upon the nature of the crop. In an undeveloped economy like that of Africa, it may be right to say that with common use of hoes and ploughs, on hundred acres of yams, cassava, or rice can create employment for perhaps twenty gainfully employed people. Most of the women and their families are unproductive workers for many reasons. They lack the training or the necessary resources to enable them to be productive as agriculturists and also may not have the possibility of acquiring such resources.

3. National incomes are often unequal. During times of rising prices, those prices paid by women tend to rise more slowly than do the prices they receive. While in the same period, the prices paid to the rural farms tend to remain fairly stable. Let us examine some of the

values about the economic system which are held by the women and other rural groups that give them political support:

a) The first value appears to be that rural farmers have inequality of income with the non-agricultural sector of the economy.
b) The second value is that the non-rural people wield stronger concentration of economic power than do rural farms. This is to the disadvantage of women. The rural women cannot reduce production on the short run, while non-farm people reduce their production in the face of declining demand. During times of economic decline, farmers' feelings regarding these matters run particularly high against marketing agencies or marketing board (price assistance fund).

A common sign of inequality in prices and income can be seen on women's outcries for the improvement of their economic and social conditions.

4. The last value held by women and rural development planners is the one that women leaders term "women fundamentalism." It is the practical difficulties that most women have to contend with. Many men fail to gain certain understanding of the social changes that are taking place among women. In addition to these values regarding rural development and women in the general economy, there is also the one held by most researchers and scholars. They maintain that the only way that women can embrace all the benefits of rural development and there by assure their position in the economy, is through government intervention to eliminate those disparities which dishonor their status and which give advantages to the males. (9)

Action Needed from the Zimbabwean Government

The government should revise laws and administrative practices to ensure women's rights to economic resources in the rural areas. Legal services and legal literacy should be made available to rural women farmers at minimal cost. Revise legislation and administrative laws to give rural market women full access to the right to inheritance and ownership of the land and other property, credit natural resources and appropriate technologies.

Citations

1. Agricultural Extension for Women in Zimbabwe 1991. A group of rural Zimbabwean women defined what means to be a woman as is: worker, organizer, manager, assistant and nurse for the home, family, community and the Nation. p. 1.2 and 2.2 http:fadr.msu.ru/roda.Ve/txt/vol16/2art6html.

2. Fourth World Conference on Women in Beijing 4-25. September, 1995.

3. Sylvester, Christine. "Gender" Zimbabwe *The Terrain of Contradictory Development* West View Press, 1992, p. 143-152. (65.6023.5y5). Sylvester discusses the debate over the gender issue in Zimbabwe. The author talks about the matrilineal power of the society and how women are affected. Yet despite the matrilineal risen to increase women's awareness of their human rights.

4. Sylvester, Christine "Gender"

5. Burdett, Marcia M. "The Role of Women in Zambia" *Between Two Worlds* West View Press 1988 p. 56 (65.9.B89) The author talks about how women are valued members of society even though they are prohibited from taking outspoken or individualistic roles.

6. Fourth World Conference on Women in Beijing. (4-25 September 1995) and the parallel NGO Forum on Women 1995 (30 August-8 September)

7. Fourth World Conference on Women in Beijing. 1995.

8. Christine Obbo, African Women, *Their Struggle for Economic Independence* ZED Press, 57 Caledonian Rd., London 1980.

9. Fourth World Conference on Women in Beijing. 1995.

Chapter 4

Urbanization and Women's Work

This chapter gives us an outline of the activities that women living in the urban areas of Zimbabwe are involved in, in order to equip themselves economically, and the problems they face on a day to day basis.

Women were selected randomly from the urban settings. Geographical distribution ranked from:

Harare
Mutare
Marondera
Gweru
Chinhoi
Chegutu
Bulawayo
Bindura
Major cities in Zimbabwe

Among those women chosen and interviewed were:

Domestic workers
Housewives
Married women
Single mothers

The stories in this chapter were recorded by the author during interview time using a tape recorder.

Some of the women chosen in this study never heard of the women's movement in Zimbabwe, but they have created their own patterns for emancipation and in the process are spearheading social change for better or for worse.

It has been said that the modern city is the place where the change in status of African women can be best observed. Women who have just arrived in town can barely look after themselves. Often they cannot find work even as domestics given the colonial habits still very much alive, of using male help, both in public places and in private houses. Also, working as a maid, particularly in public places, is deemed a "dirt job" bound to lead to prostitution and suitable only for unschooled women who have to keep themselves and their children after being deserted by their husbands or lovers. (1)

Even educated women who are aspiring to office work, which is the popular female occupation in towns, often have to face blackmail from their employers, only too ready to claim sexual favors in return for providing work. (2)

Clearly migrant women find themselves tackling urban labor form a position of extreme social weakness. True, in the traditional society, as a field laborer on behalf of her husband, she would necessarily combine work and sexual services, nevertheless, she had greater social strength and security and some bargaining power.

The spectrum of prostitution and the fear of loss of the head of the family prestige makes urban males unreservedly, hostile to any extra-domestic occupation of their wives.

Labor in the Suburbs

On a sunny Sunday afternoon in the low density town suburbs of Harare, many women sit on the pavements. They sit in groups, or alone, talking and resting, making the most of the few hours they have for themselves. These women are domestic workers. Most of them are migrant workers from the rural areas. They have little or no formal education. They usually have nowhere to stay when they come to the town. So, live-in work is their only option.

Why Domestic Work?

Nyemba Dzinesu was born and brought up in Mhondoro Chivero village. Her father raised cattle and her mother worked around the house. She left school in the middle of standard four, the sixth year of schooling.

"Well, what could I do with so little education and I had to earn money because my family was so poor. All I can do is domestic work to earn some money." She explained. (3)

Anna Gumbo's parents died when she was a baby and she went to live with her grand mother in Chegutu. When she finished standard two, she left school. "I wanted to become a nurse but you can't do that with little education. The only thing I could do was housework. I looked for work around Chegutu but there were no jobs so I came to Harare. I did not know anyone here so I had nowhere to stay. I walked around every day looking for a job, and in the night I slept anywhere. The good thing about this job is that you get somewhere to stay." (4)

Because women can live-in at the place of work, domestic service in Zimbabwe, unlike Britain or United States has remained a full-time rather than a part-time occupation. But economic recession means that many employers can no longer afford the services of a full-time domestic worker. Employers do their own housework, or employ someone once a week. So, domestic workers have been forced to find several different jobs for different days of the week (piece work). Piece work is a difficult way to earn a living. Full-time work generally pays better than part-time work and offers the additional perk of free board and lodging. It is also difficult for women to find a job for every day of the week.

Families of Domestic Workers

Most domestic workers have homes and families in the rural areas. To support the family the domestic worker must send most of her wages home. Low wages make it very difficult for domestic workers to support their families. Many are single parents. Others are married but their husbands seldom give them money.

Kate Zimbwa has three children in Mosva Village, Chivero, who are being looked after by her mother and an old uncle. She earns $200 per month and sends most of it home. "It is a big struggle for me because I don not have a husband. So there is no one to help me with money and I want my children to finish school and get good jobs."(5)

Daily Life of the Domestic Worker

Domestic work is tedious and tiring. Workers start work early and finish late. If they "live in," they may always be on call. They can be asked to baby-sit, make tea, or run up to the shops, even when they are not on duty. The job usually includes: cleaning washing, ironing, cooking, as well as looking after children.

Nyembezi Ngini said, "I work very hard. I must start work at six o'clock in the morning and only finish at 8:30 p.m., after they have finished eating supper and I have washed up the dishes. Every Friday I have to work until 10:00 p.m. because my madam and master go out. I do not get paid any extra money for doing it." (6)

Time Off for Domestic Workers

Unlike factory work, domestic work has no strict laws which set the hours of work, leave, or terms of contract. These arrangements are usually laid down by the employer. A domestic worker's hours and time off depend on her employer's lifestyle. Time off, which includes time off during the week and annual leave, is usually arranged so that the employer is not inconvenienced. However, minimum wage level laws have been put in place by the government regarding hours of work and time off.

The Informal Economy
Petty Trades: Women-Urban

Some women receive and collect the goods from the interior, and carry them to the various markets for sale to retailers. Many women exhibit their merchandise on the premises in front of their houses, on stones, barrels, and trestle tables. They trade cigarettes, matches, sweets, and vegetables, as well as cosmetics, which are their best selling items.

This kind of trade leaves the wife time to work at her domestic occupation while customers can be served by other members of the family.

Cross-Border Trading

Cross-border trading is increasingly a women's domain, and presupposes great financial means. Women travel by buses and trains, mainly to South Africa, Botswana, Malawi, and Mozambique to sell crocheted goods, and various other crafts, and then return with hi-tech goods to sell on the home market. This type of trading has improved a lot of women's lives in Zimbabwe. It has also contributed to the economy of Zimbabwe.

If you walk in the streets and the shops, you will find all sorts of goods from neighboring countries. Crossing the border is not an easy thing for the Zimbabwean women. Sometimes they face harassment by the customs officers in both countries. Some women have even lost their lives on their way to South Africa.

"Prepared Foods" Vendors

Selling prepared foods is one of the activities that is popular among women in Zimbabwe towns. The women focus on the industrial areas where there are laborers and office clerks, but still they cannot supply the demands of all the workers by themselves.

Most women reconnoiter an area first, making arrangements with a group of workers for particular kinds of dishes. Other women just appear at places and, if the workers like the food, they would come again. As for the type of food a particular woman might supply, this would in most cases reflect the staple diet or ethnic cooking of the vendor.

Many vendors buy their supplies every day from suppliers outside the big retail market at Mbare Musika at a lower price. They have to be there as early as 6:00 a.m. and be prepared to bargain at times.

These women use wheelbarrows or carry the food on their heads. The cooking is sometimes done outside or in an outside shelter which is much safer from the point of view of starting a fire but more dangerous for children playing nearby.

Having fed the children and transferred the food into suitable receptacles, the women would set off for her destination, getting there by 12:30 or 1:00 p.m. in time for the 30 minute lunch breaks. Plates are scarce and customers are sometimes asked o bring their own.

The food is sold for cash only, at prices determined by the vendors. The prices depend on the food served and the vendor. A plate full will cost normally $3.00. Vendors make a net profit of $200 to $300 a month.

Like most businesses, success depends upon hard work. The food business is now very competitive and women are constantly expanding their markets.

A food vendor's association was formed. This association includes men and women. The aim of the association is to try and secure trade licenses for members, and to request managers to allow them to sell food in the firms or on factory premises.

The City Council licensing and law enforcement officers deny licenses to sell food for public health reasons, but they are aware that these women food hawkers are selling illegally.

The Council officers have decided to close their eyes to the practice, first of all because the women service government employees, including the law enforcers themselves. As a result the women food sellers are left alone while snack and soft drink vendors are frequently prosecuted for littering the city and trading in the wrong places.

The Informal Sector

Between the security of a regular job and the despair of total unemployment is the informal sector. Zimbabwean women earn their living by sewing, buying and selling, or running shebeens.

Many unemployed women drift into informal sector activities. At first it is a stop-gap while they are still looking for jobs. Then as the search becomes more difficult, the informal sector becomes a permanent way of earning money.

The informal sector is often romanticized. The virtues of enterprise and hard work and the ideal of the self-made man have been held up as a result of informal sector activity. For unemployed and often elderly women, the informal sector offers very little.

The following people show vividly, the great effort that provides small rewards:

Media Chinyemba said, "I make money by selling beers. A dozen costs $8.00 and I normally buy four dozen. Each is sold at 90 cents. I use a refrigerator to cool them and I buy a liter of paraffin at 63 cents. My customers buy them and take them away. Some customers spend the day up to 8 p.m. At times we get arrested and the fine is $100 and our stock gets confiscated. There is no place you can claim the confiscation. I have been selling beer for five years. It is better when you work because this business is not always profitable. At times there are no customers and; you might end up not having sold a thing throughout the week. The profit is $50 or$60 week, depending on how I sold. This includes the brandy and the spirits." (7)

Many informal sector activities are illegal. Police harassment is a constant worry for many women.

Letiwina Mezi said, "I make money by selling spinach, rape, cabbage, and maize to the people. In order to get these I have to travel by car to farms or Mbare Musika. A trip is $6.00 depending on the distance. If it is very far it could cost more. For the vegetables, the charge is $2.00 or $5.00 a bundle. When reselling I do not make much profit. I sell from an open space. Police used to harass us before, but of late they have stopped. I have applied for a license but I was told to wait. I m still waiting, but I and other people have asked to be given a chance without harassment, because it is not a fault of ours that the licenses are never ready. But we must live and how will we survive? I have been doing this on and off since 1976, when my elder daughter was still at school. It is not the best, but I can still help myself out. After all, if the money is deducted I make a profit of $10 a day." (8)

Because profits are so low the women have to account for every cent spent. Other women see the informal sector work as a supplement to money that they get from other sources.

Neta Moyo said, "I make money by selling pillow cases and sheets. Normally I buy for $20 and a profit would be $10 every week per stock. I have been doing this for ten years. It is worse if I spend $20 on materials and the $10 gain cannot come up to all my demands. But for the meantime it is better because it is just an addition to what my boyfriend offers." (9)

The Unemployed Women

With rapidly increasing unemployment there are groups of people who are especially vulnerable. Young people, women, and those restricted to rural areas come off worst.

It is almost impossible to find accurate statistics on general unemployment in Zimbabwe. In the case of women the task is even more difficult. The reason is that state statistics define unemployment as those who have recently lost their jobs and are actively seeking new work. Otherwise "unemployment" refers to people registered at the government labor bureau as "work seekers." (10)

Housewives are classified as "not economically active." This hides the time, energy, and labor that goes into looking after households. Women may often have to choose between staying home to look after the children, or working while leaving them alone at home.

Many women leave work or are fired because of ill health. Nyaradzo Mwendamberi said, "I am unemployed. I have been working at Julie White fashions. Because of a stroke in 1988, I left that job. I have been without a job for nine years. I felt bad leaving because I liked my job. It was a light job, dispatching and receiving goods. I am looking for a job, but not far away from my home because I still have a problem with my foot. I can not move fast or for a long distance. I look for jobs by applying, but there is nothing. (11)

The long search for work is a depressing experience for many women. Women work-seekers interviewed in a survey in Harare used a number of methods. The first was to go door to door, from factory to factory, and shop to shop. Many of the women found this to be an expensive and unsatisfactory method of finding work.

These are some of the stories from the survey:

Tsitsi Soko said, "I usually look for a job through door to door. It is hard to get a job because when you get to a place looking for a job, you can never know whether that is a good place to look for a job, or may be it could be a place where people get killed. You, the one in need, you just go in and at times the boss just says 'I don't need People.' One has to move out disappointed because you were with the hope of being employed." (12)

The most common way to find work is to ask friends and relatives to look for vacancies at their workplace. Four of the women in that area had found work in this way. Other women felt that this was unfair. They felt at a disadvantage if they did not have personal contact in a workplace. Anna Kapfidze, a 45 year old woman said, "It is hard to find a job because one finds that there are many people in the lines for jobs, so it is difficult to be picked up from that lot." (13)

"I once went to Parirenyatwa hospital looking for a job as a cleaner," she continued, "and was told by the Superintendent that I was too old. Since then I have not looked for work."

A last attempt of finding work is to go to the labor bureau on Kambuzuma Road in Harare, to line up and wait for the clerks to come and call you one by one. It means to be the first one you have to wake up early and if not, you do not get anything.

Sara Kapito had a similar experience with the labor bureau. "I live through marketing and I also look for a job by going to Kambuzuma Road. I always report in those offices at 7 a.m. and stand in queue. The clerks will call us one by one to the office if there is a job they can offer. When you are called inside, you might get it, but usually not and you are unfortunate. At times you are given a card with a number on it in rotation as they call it. It is hard to find a job you want through that system. It would be a question of luck." (14)

Chipo Ngoni said, "It is hard to get a job because many factories are retrenching and there are a lot of people who are looking for jobs."

Many of the women felt guilty because they did not have a job and so could not help their families.

Tozivepi Kadye said, "It is now a year since I have had no job. I am actively looking for a job. Since a lot of people are unemployed, I do not mind doing any kind of job. As long as I work and get something to help my husband in maintaining the children." (15)

Some of the women felt depressed about being unemployed. "Unemployment has brought me loneliness and frustration. My husband divorced me because I had lost a job. The whole day when all my family members are away at work I stay alone and there isn't enough money. Sometimes I stay without money for the whole month until my daughter comes in to give me something," said Mary Koroka. (16)

Statistics define women living in rural areas as subsistence agricultural producers and so they are not counted among the unemployed. (17)

Access to land or not, the majority of rural women are unable to exist without some form of cash income. Like their urban sisters, once these women have had a job and lost it, it is extremely difficult to find another.

Summary

Women's participation in remunerated work in the formal and non-formal labour market has increased significantly and has changed during the past decade

Women have also become increasingly involved in micro, small, and medium sized enterprises, and in some cases, have become more dominant in the expanding informal sector.

However, women have been particularly affected by the economic situation and restructuring processes, which have changed the nature of employment and in some cases have led to the loss of jobs, even for professional and skilled women.

In addition, many women have entered the informal sector owing to the lack of other opportunities. Although some women have advanced in economic structures, for the majority of women, particularly those who face additional barriers, continuing obstacles have hindered their ability to achieve economic autonomy and to ensure sustainable livelihoods for themselves and their dependants. Women are active in a variety of economic areas, which they often combine, ranging from wage labor, and subsistence farming, to the informal sector.

However, legal and customary barriers to ownership of or access to land, natural resources, capital, credit, technology and other means of production as well as wage differentials, contributed to development not only through remunerated work but also through a great deal of unremunerated work. On the one hand women participate in the production of goods and services for the market and house hold consumption, in agriculture, food production or family enterprises.

The skills of women, if better utilized, could constitute a major contribution to the economic life of Zimbabwe. Their input should continue to be developed and supported and their potential further realized.

Citations

1. Sylvester, Christine "Gender" Zimbabwe: The Terrain of Contradictory Development West View Press, 1992.
2. Njoku, John E. Eberegbula m—*The World of the African Woman.* Copyright 1980 by John E. Eberegbulam Njoku in United Sates of America.
3. Interview in Hatfield suburb at 4 Brown Close, Harare at the residence of Stephen and Christine Chivima 1997.
4. Interview in Highlands suburb at 10 Aintree Road Highlands at the residence of David and Abinah Chapfika 1997.
5. Interview in Chegutu City in 1997.
6. Interview in Gweru at the residence of one of the General Managers of OK chain Stores.
7. Interview at Mbare Flats, Harare in 1997.
8. Interview at Kuwadzana high density suburb in 1997.
9. Interview at Bulawayo City at Luveve Township 1997.
10. Employment Bureau, Harare 1993.
11. Employment Bureau, Harare 1997.
12. Interview in Harare 1997.
13. Interview in High field 1997.
14. Interview in Harare 1997.
15. Interview in Harare 1997.
16. Interview in Harare 1997
17. Rural development and Women in Africa. International labor office, Geneva HQ1240.5 A35 R 87 1986.

Chapter 5

Women and Employment

The gradual change from family production of goods and services to specialized production has occurred simultaneously with the evolution from an agricultural base to a technological and manufacturing base supported by a service sector. The roles of both men and women in society and in the work place have changed radically as a result of these transitions. In many parts of the Third World, changing from an agriculturally based economy to a market economy has forced men, women, and children to exchange labor for money with which to purchase basic necessities.(1) Subsequently more women are making the transition from the home to the workplace to supplement family incomes. The nuclear family unit is also evolving as many women are becoming the sole family income earners or as their spouses migrate to look for work or leave them for other women. With limited work skills, low levels of education and doors closing in the formal sector, women have to create their own employment in the informal sector. (Peeble 1984)

Paid employment is a key issue for women. Women's social and political status is closely linked to their economic status, as their incomes increase. Women in most societies have more political and social value attributed to them. It suffices to say that women's access to income generating activities is an essential step toward achieving economic independence. Economic independence can provide an opportunity to become more aware of the workings of the larger economic literacy is a means of empowerment for women in a world where capitalism is predominant.

Adult education is an approach that can be used to develop a curriculum that enhances this aforementioned step. (2) In looking at improving economic opportunities for women, the educational process can only be understood if it is located in the geographical setting, economic and political system, social stratum, and community group of the learners or the participants will not engage themselves in the learning process because it will have no place in their lives.(3)

It is therefore critical that local experiences be utilized, as curriculum for the participants in any program that facilitates a learning process assisting women to move into the public sphere of the economy.(4)

Despite the allegation that women lack qualification, I see women around the regions of Matebeleland, Manicaland, and Mashonaland who are well educated, exceedingly competent, dedicated to their employers or their professions, really working hard, confident of their own skills and abilities, and of course increasingly ambitious. Yet, in spite of all these personal and professional qualifications they are still not being considered on a par with men. That particular disease is alive and thriving in our society.

The other side of the coin is that there is a certain knowledge men have that women seem not to have, that is, information about the business world. The business world as it exists now and as it is being redesigned for the new economic situation of the 1980's was developed by men for men, so they understand it. In one respect, then, management men are right, most women are unqualified in the sense that they know nothing about how business or government or academia operate at the top administrative or managerial level. As women they have been totally excluded from that kind of experience. (5) Instead of recognizing what the source of women's problems actually is, women tend to look for weaknesses within themselves. Women are advised to deal with their anxieties and guilt and to examine their motivations for working.

When did you last hear of any man asked to explain his motivations for working at a job interview? When are men asked what they really want to do in this world? When are they instructed to make endless lists of goals?

Women are under utilized in the world of work. Today 39% of the total labor force is women, yet only about 1% of them reach the upper levels of management on the top of their profession. (6) The participation rate of women between the ages of 16 to 65 is a startling 43.4%, but the success measures, when compared to male is less than comforting.(7) The pay gap is more than $3,000 per year on the average. The unemployment rate for women is higher than for men, and the largest percent of working women are found in lower paying jobs.(8) Facts are facts, but the big questions is why? Zimbabwe is experiencing a period of awakening, laws barring discrimination on any basis have been passed, yet women continue to experience real barriers in the world of work. Rather than merely point a finger and shout male chauvinism, women need to take a hard look at the interplay of a variety of factors which influence women.

The societal image of women in African culture seems to be bounded by two dimensions. Women are viewed primarily as sex objects and as servants. As a result of these two dimensional scales, from birth the process of socialization processes emphasize independence, work, and career orientation for males, and dependency and sex orientation for women. Researchers have repeatedly shown this in a variety of ways. The way children are responded to by their parents, the kinds of toys that are chosen for them, the role taking within the family in imitative acts, and hundreds of ways of channels that occur within the family long before the child is of school age.(9)

Children's literature is replete with examples emphasizing dependency and sexism for women. Based on this culture view of the role of women, we move easily into a set of basic assumptions differentiating the sexes. Assumptions about the physical and psychological differences are easily formed e.g. "women are weak." This may be true if we are talking about grip, or other forms of muscular exertion. However in a statistical sense, we know that more males than females are born, but that more females survive, and their life expectancy exceeds men's by several years. Males are assumed to be aggressive, thing oriented, and independent. Females are assumed to be passive, sensitive, dependent, and people oriented.

Acting on the basis of these assumptions, relationships are patterned and socialization continues. There is evidence to refute these assumptions but we tend to ignore it. Intellectual and cognitive ability, inherent differences in the sexes, are non existent. In spite of this, the cultural concept of women's roles continues, the circular reasoning which contributes to the inability of women to maximize their potential. Women tend to have a negative image of their own self worth. They are constantly reminded that the woman's role is passive and non-assertive. Physical attractiveness, sensitivity, and service are dominant modes reflecting the two dimensional axis of sexuality and servitude mentioned earlier.

Girls are constantly advised against risk taking and urged to take the safe sure ways. Their educational process seldom emphasizes leadership and team work roles for women. The individual female who is independent enough to make a decision for her, to take a risk, or to go contrary to the culture, is seldom made to assume the consequences of her decision if they are unpleasant. Because she lacks conviction of her own ability, she tends to undermine her own self confidence. Because she fails to expose herself, she develops a pattern of avoidance of risk taking. Because her motivation is otherwise directed, she fails to set goals for herself and plan how to achieve them. The result is low achievement motivation. Because she fails to set goals and plans, she doesn't seek, she doesn't prepare, and she doesn't achieve. Lack of achievement helps to contribute to her own feeling of inferiority and leads her right back to where she started-dependent, passive, and ambivalent.

Women are assigned roles in the culture emphasizing dependency. Mothers provide a role image primarily of the servant model. They also encourage participation and imitation of the following models: they cook, bake, clean, chauffeur, nurse, garden, and shop. All of these activities include an element of service to others. At the same time mothers begin the process of emphasis in the sexual role. They emphasize personal appearance, posture, and behavior intended to attract interest and attention. The role models continue through the school years. Teachers are women, administrators are men. Boys are athletes, girls are cheerleaders. Boys take shop, and girls take home economics.

As career choice time approaches, girls are channeled into nursing, boys into medicine, girls to dental hygiene, boys to dentistry, girls to service industries, boys to skill trades, and on and on. What happens when females approach the boundaries of expected behavior for their roles?

First, they are censured, "nice girls don't do that." Then they are ridiculed, "our tomboy daughter, she prefers football to dolls." Then they are discouraged, "go into nursing, the training is shorter and girls will never succeed in medical school." Then she is denied, "We can't afford college for you, since your brother will be away at engineering school, why not take typing and get a job?" Her need to achieve is gently sublimated to a need to nurture and serve. She is discouraged and protected from taking risks by her parents. At the same time, she is subjected to peer pressure to fit the mold, "if you take chemistry you won't have time to date," and on and on. So she doesn't plan for the long range, and doesn't recognize choice points, but begins to back into or avoid decision making. She becomes more dependent on others because it is easy and comfortable. She ceases her formal education, takes a job, finds a man, and becomes the role model.

More than half of the high school graduates are women, but the percentage receiving degrees for advanced study drops sharply as the degrees for advanced levels progress (41% Bachelor Degrees, 37% Masters Degrees, and 11% of Doctoral Degrees).

Women lack acquaintance with leader roles and team work. Given a choice between equally qualified female and male bosses, the usual choice is male. Sex may be part of the choice, but the actual fact is that many women do not know how to lead effectively, do not know how to plan, organize and control, do not know how to use their analytical ability to pinpoint problem areas and screen alternatives, do not know how to make decisions and do not know how to activate after decisions.

Factors within the Organizations

The total staffing process within an organization is a reflection of the individual and combined assumptions of female roles. Recruitment and section practices tend to favor males. Many decisions are based on myths that continue to exist and which reflect the sex and service axis. Examples are: women do not need to work; women can be paid less because they are supported by husbands and fathers.

Selection, placement, training, and reward, reflect these assumptions. A job description may be stated in objective terms. It describes a job to be accomplished. The specification of qualities and skills necessary to (successfully) perform the job often are also objectively stated. However, objective statements may be interpreted subjectively during the recruitment and selection process. Recruitment may centre in predominantly male colleges for managerial trainees. Selection may be based on the assumption of performance or impermanence of the prospective candidates. These practices are not deliberate and intentionally sexist, but are often inadvertent reflections of the attitudinal beliefs of the employer.

Once an individual has been hired, the question of placement becomes paramount. Women tend to be channeled into dead end jobs. They are not often found in positions that have direct lines of progression to top management jobs. A woman is not expected to be a long time employee. She is not thought of as career oriented. Women help contribute to this myth in two ways. They themselves are not achievement oriented and they do not have the confidence in themselves to aggressively seek recognition and promotion. Women also fail to support one another in the sense of pulling together as a team. So, competent females are steered into jobs of servitude and fail to recognize or accept that fact.

The bosses "girl Friday," and the "strong right arm," are usual roles for women in the industry. Salary scales are notable less for women than men.

Again a reflection of women's worth by men, and acceptance of a lack of worth on women's part.

In countless organizations, women are placed in "assistant to" categories rather than assistant status. The inclusion of the word "to" in a title is a clear indication of two things: poor pay, and lack of independence in decision making and action. The "assistant to" never makes decisions or takes action in her own right, but always acts as a representative of her boss, while the "assistant" acts in his or her own right.

Training and development opportunities are an almost exclusive male prerogative in organizations. Women contribute to this phenomenon by not actively seeking opportunities to increase their ability and status. Promotional opportunities are often overlooked by females. They do not approve of other women breaking the role parameters. One way to promotion resides in the sponsorship of one higher in the organization. It is difficult for both the sponsor and the woman he is sponsoring, for a variety of reasons. The foremost one is the sexual connotation implied by others. Another strong one is the servant one if the sponsor supports his "strong right arm," he will lose her services and deprive himself. It is also difficult for a woman to get tapped into the informal communication and power structure of the organization.

A final area of leadership in organizations that mitigates against women is the area of decision making and action. Most decision making involves some risk taking. Women have not been taught the skills necessary to state problems, consider alternatives, and make decisions.

They have been taught skills in diagnosis, but lack the emphasis on skill pattern of decision. They do not command respect, and they do not understand or exercise leadership qualities. They are not independent enough to exercise choice and assume the responsibilities that result from action. The implicit assumption in the African culture is that change, when it concerns women's roles, is risk. Women are often presented with ambiguous signals from men in order to curb rapid social change. There are fears and doubts about women changing their roles, in particular, women's increasing participation in political and economic life.

The result is often that women become defensive and even begin to doubt the desirability of change, preferring the security of tradition, which at least does not cause increased anxiety.

While men in Zimbabwe urge women to march forward with them, women's interest are often perceived as in conflict with their own. Elite women frequently actually support the men when patriarchal opinions, preventing women from speaking out on issues of social and economic change, are spiced with nationalistic sentiments. Some men feel strongly that women abuse the privilege of working, becoming too big-headed to accept the superior position accorded to men by the bible, supporting this view with the fact that young girls are reluctant to return to the villages, while married women desert or divorce their husbands.

In any event, many women wind up as prostitutes. It is not clear why self-supporting is so often fulfilled by prostitution. However, women caught between the past and the present are not fulfilling their culturally expected role when they do not cultivate the land and feed their families as their mothers did. It is not surprising that Zimbabwean urban women are stereotyped as wasting money on expensive clothes and beauty products while their children suffer from Kwashiorkor, a protein deficiency caused by ignorance of the principles of nutrition which occurs in both the rural and urban areas.

It in fact illustrates the misplaced priorities that lead women to engage in conspicuous consumption at the expense of their family's health. However, the men prefer to blame the women for failing in their role as food providers, especially if the women live in the towns. It is argued that women cannot do justice to domestic work and child rearing while simultaneously engaged in wage labor. This provides additional support for the argument that the solution to male unemployment is the sacking of all employed women who are selfish enough to hold other jobs in addition to marriage. This view ignores the fact that women without a separate income are subject to whims of men who may withhold support from their families while spending their money on drinking or other women.

Women who work not only ward off starvation but they reduce that kind of unhealthy dependence. In Zimbabwean society women are constantly reminded, "the pride of a proper woman is a husband," with the warning that they may miss out on this blessing or fulfillment through insufficient submissiveness. Spinsters and divorcees, are said to owe their status to challenging male supremacy, particularly so if the women are educated.

In all this seems to be a refusal on the part of men to accept the changes taking place in society as a whole, and a misinterpretation of the real purpose of education. There has been a lot of debate concerning the effects of female education upon marital stability. A lot of men expressed great indignation against women who believed that education meant emancipation and equality with men. Some men in Zimbabwe attempt to solve this problem by marrying women with little or no education, whom they hope to impress; and control by virtue of their superior station in society.

However, this rarely works as the education gap proves either unbridgeable or a problem in itself. Three things happen: the women are neglected when, either the men turn to the town women whom in other contexts they categories as prostitutes, or when they turn to the more educated women from whom they attempted to escape originally, or when husbands attempt to educate the women under their own guidance and supervision. However, as soon as women acquire some occupational skills, they want to work. The right to work can result in full or partial economic independence which enables women to make their own decisions.

But however minimal women's successes are, many men resent them despite the desirability of a second income to maintain the high living standard of the elites, which have made women's employment acceptable even to men who previously would have prevented the employment of their wives in the public sector.

In addition, the expansion of the informal sector which depends primarily upon the individual initiative has lessened the male monopoly on making decisions about whether women should work. "Women these days are not controllable," is the constant complaint of Zimbabwean men with regards to women's employment. Fear and frustration in personal or professional relationships with individual women lead men to lash out at all women, particularly those in wage employment. Any attempt at self-reliance and economic independence is interpreted a challenge to male juridical supremacy and therefore bad for African society.

Most men expect the impossible from educated women who will blindly obey their wishes and who will stay in the rural areas cultivating food. The good woman stays in the village because if she goes to town she is a source of worry for her husband. In Zimbabwe there is a tendency to regard all urban women as sexually loose, especially any who work or appear well dressed. Thus, prejudice is extended by the general populace even to highly educated women attempting to enter professions.

As well as arguing that "a woman's place is in the home," in order to reduce female competition for taxpayer's jobs, lovers and husbands positively resent the employment of women because it brings them in contact with other men and affords them some degree of economic independence. The men want to have the best of both worlds, the urban and the traditional, and they produce elaborate rationalizations to justify themselves. Men regard it as their duty to tackle the hostile, westernized, urban environment and to protect their women from it. In other words, men can work for wages in towns, but women can only do so at the cost of moral corruption.

The Private Sector

Lack of employment in the private sector and reductions in public sector service jobs have affected women disproportionately. In Zimbabwe, women take on more unpaid work, such as the care of children and those who are ill or elderly, compensating for lost household income particularly when public services are not available. In many cases, employment creation strategies have not paid sufficient attention to occupations and sectors where women predominate, nor have they adequately promoted the access of women to those occupations and sectors that are traditionally male.

For those women who are employed, many experience obstacles that prevent them from achieving their potential. While some are increasingly found in lower levels of management, attitudinal discrimination often prevents them from being promoted further.

The experience of sexual harassment is an affront to a worker's dignity and prevents women from making a contribution commensurate with their abilities. The lack of a family friendly work environment, as well as inflexible working hours, further prevents women from achieving their potential. In the private sector, including transitional and national enterprises, women are largely absent from management and policy levels, denoting discriminatory hiring and promotion policies and practices. The unfavorable work environment, as well as the limited number of employment opportunities available, has led many women to seek alternatives. Women have increasingly become self-employed, and owners and mangers of micro, small, and medium—scale enterprises.

The expansion of the informal sector in the country, and of self-organized and independent enterprises, is in large part due to women whose collaborative self-help and traditional practices initiatives in production and trade represent a vital economic resource. When they gain access to and control over capital, credit, and other resources, including technology and training, women can increase production, marketing, and income for sustainable development.

In addressing the economic potential and independence of women, the government of Zimbabwe and other actors should promote an active and visible policy of mainstreaming a gender perspective in all policies and programs, so that before decisions are taken, an analysis is made of the effects on women and men, respectively.

Action to be considered by
Government and Policy-Makers of Zimbabwe

Guarantee the rights of women and men to equal pay for equal work or work of equal value. Implement laws against discrimination based on sex in the labor market, especially considering older women workers, hiring and promotion, the extension of employment benefits and social security, and working condition. Ensure equal access of women to effective job training, retraining, counseling, and placement services that are not limited to traditional employment areas. Ensure equal access of women to ongoing training in the workplace, including unemployed women, single parents, women re-entering the labor market after an extended temporary exit from employment owing to family responsibilities and other causes, and women displaced by new forms of production or by retrenchment, and increase incentives to enterprises to expand the number of vocational and training centers that provide training for women in non-traditional areas.

Provide affordable support services, such as high quality, flexible and affordable child care services that take into account the needs of working women. Adopt policies to extend or maintain the protection of labor laws and social security provisions for those who do paid work in the home. The private sector, including transitional and national corporations must recruit women for leadership and training programs, all on an equal basis with men. They must recognize collective bargaining as a right and as an important mechanism for eliminating wage inequality for women and to improve working conditions. Promote the election of women trade union officials and ensure that trade union officials elected to represent women are given job protection and physical security in connection with the discharge of their functions. Ensure access to, and develop special programs that enable women with disabilities to obtain and retain employment, and ensure access to education and training at all proper levels. In accordance with the standard rules on equalization of opportunities for persons with disabilities, adjust working conditions to the extent possible, in order to suit the needs of women with disabilities, who should be assured legal protection against unfounded job loss on account of their disabilities. Review, analyze, and where appropriate, reformulate the wage structure in female dominated professions, such as teaching, nursing, and child care with a view to raising their low status earnings. (10)

Citations

1. Women, Work, and Gender Relations in Developing Countries—A Perspective. Edited by Parvin Ghorayshi and Claire Belanger 1240. W6659 p.14.
2. Women, Work, and Gender p. 14.
3. Women, Work, and Gender p. 196.
4. Women, Work, and Gender p. 196.
5. Christine Obbo, *African Women, Their Struggle for Economic Independence.*
6. Maria Rosa, Women of Africa *Roots of Oppression* by Faro Buonoparte 52, 20121 Milani, first published in English and updated edition by Zed Press, 57 Caledonian Rd., London N19 DN.
7. Maria Rosa, Roots of Oppression.
8. Christine Obbo, African Women.
9. Njoku, John E. Eberegbulan—*The World of the African Woman,* copyright 1980 by John Eberegbulan Njoku in United States of America.
10. "Women in Politics" for National Preparatory Committee—Beijing 1995. 1980

Chapter 6

Women in Business—Entrepreneurs

The African woman as entrepreneur is not a twentieth century phenomenon, but an aspect of reality deeply rooted in the history of African social, economic, and political structures. (1) There were local community marketplaces where most of the local food stuffs, crafts, and a few necessaries were sold. Current perceptions and role definitions of African female entrepreneurs grow out of this historical pattern of development. Consequently, the pervasive image of the entrepreneur is that of street vendor and market trader. On the other hand, there is also a small but emerging group of business women who are proprietors of developing industrial enterprises and retail shops. This is a group for which there is little or no systematic data and analysis, yet its existence and economic activities require a broader perspective concerning the parameters of entrepreneurship. Specifically, "entrepreneur" refers to any independent or self-employed person who controls the management of capital and who invests it in some enterprise to gain profit.

In Africa's urban areas and rural commercial centers, women play predominant roles as traders. (2) Operating in what is known as the "parallel" or "informal" markets, these women are generally self-employed entrepreneurs with tremendous business acumen. They operate in wholesale and retail distribution industries, often providing the key market access for primary manufactured goods as well as food.

The institutions that women have created and the parallel market which they have come to dominate has become major employers in both urban and rural areas, not just for women but for men as well. Despite the fact that most existing policies aimed at economic reform are focused at increasing the financial capacity and stimulating economic activity within the formal sector, it is the informal sector which has managed to thrive and indeed grow during the last five years of structural adjustment. Indeed, these reforms have had very little impact on the informal sector except in some cases to push commercial activity into this parallel market. Most women are in the primary industry in the agricultural sector, with the remainder distributed in the secondary and tertiary non-agricultural labor force. The majority of women in the latter are in the service sector, where they are over-represented in self-employment retail trade, and earn a living and cash income by working independently.

Zimbabwean Women—Scale of Activity

Women dominate the retail trade, whether in the marketplace, on the streets, or on the premises of their compounds. They are under represented in wholesale and import trading and in other large scale businesses that are handled and controlled by both Zimbabwean and non-Zimbabwean men. There is an increasing number of women industrialists, but little is known about the range and limits of their economic activity. Moreover, there exists a small but significant group of "market queens," whose business activities have taken on international dimensions.

Female dominance in market centers is well established in West Africa, Zimbabwe, Zambia, and Malawi up to this date. (3) Thus, while the general trading organization is that of the one person enterprise, the scale of female entrepreneurship varies from those engaged in the (wholesale), retail, productive and distributive processes, to those engaged in extremely small scale local street hawking, or market gardening and vending. The range of economic activity expands across all industrial sectors, agriculture, manufacturing, and service.

Types of Business Activity

As commercial traders, women handle mainly food and agricultural products, fruit, vegetables, eggs, and poultry. Half of the traders deal with food stuffs, about one quarter sell various other goods, mainly manufacturers, and about one fifth more (tailors and traders in food prepared on the spot) combine processing and trading activities.

Traditionally, other self employed women engage in market gardening, poultry rearing, beer brewing, and spirit making (kachasu), hairdressing, dressmaking, and laundering. Others engage in lucrative crafts such as the making of pottery and the dyeing of cloth.

Female business proprietors work in large scale transport activities as owners of taxis, lorries and busses. There is scattered information about women who own various manufacturing and service enterprises such as hotels, food canneries and dress shops.

Income and Wealth of Entrepreneurial Women

Some of the women are wealthy and earn large incomes (running into four figures). They have penetrated the higher capital return wholesale and import market. They are few in number, and tend to work in the secondary and tertiary sector, mainly in transport, wholesale, and manufacturing. The majority of women are "petty traders" working in a highly competitive market place. They deal in a variety of goods, but in quite small quantities. Their incomes are low and their average annual profit has been estimated from a low 5 to 6 percent, to a high 20 to 30 percent of value turn over.

Age and Education of Entrepreneurial Women

The majority of women entrepreneurs have little or no education, ranging from no school at all, to only a few years of primary school. Women with higher levels of education are in larger scale business activities and tend to be better off economically. Women between the ages of 30 years and 60 years are over represented in the entrepreneurial group, which suggests a high correlation between the high rate of illiteracy and the high average age of women traders.

Locality Base of Entrepreneurial Women

Female entrepreneurship is an established reality in rural and urban areas, but the intensity and diversity of female business enterprises are more evident in the cities and urban fringe areas. The rise of tertiary industries and services is linked to the process of urbanization and the changing scale of societal activity in general. This trend does not belie the significant existence of self employed workers in villages and rural towns. The percentages for women in both villages and towns is considerably higher, and they in fact constitute more than 85 percent of all sales workers.

Perspective on the Women as Entrepreneur

Female entrepreneurs, particularly market traders, provide essential services to consumers in the urban and rural areas. They work as owners of neighborhood and community general stores, as clothiers and fashion designers, artisans and beauticians. They make goods available to the consumer in quantities the average person can afford and thereby fulfill an important public need. Women make a significant contribution to economic and social development in that they are largely responsible for the internal distribution of food and other local services. It has been acknowledged that, without the day to day initiative of traders and lorry owners, a large part of the produce would rot, the rural population would lack many modern amenities, and the main population centers would starve.

The issue, therefore, is not the exclusion of women from participation in the economic sector in most of Africa. Rather, the problem is one of concern for the character and quality of their participation, given the changing economic and social structures in different locations.

Women are subject to institutional discrimination such as unequal access to education. Economically, they receive minimal rewards. A large number of women engage in trading because there are limited economic alternatives for them to do other work. Moreover, the possibilities of broadening the range of employment opportunities depends on the extent to which there is expansion and diversification of the economy.

A number of questions are raised regarding the position of a Zimbabwean woman as entrepreneur, her changing patterns of participation, and the changing nature of societal relationships of which she is a part. The questions, most of which are fairly general and abstract, should serve as heuristic devices. Hopefully, new perspectives and programmatic ideas can be generated around the role of the female entrepreneur in development.

Barriers Women Face

Historical events form pre-colonial to post independent has had infinite repercussions in every institutional arena in which the women operate. (4) Structural transformations are reflected in changing forms of government, political leadership, economic relations and policies, cultural traditions, and style of life. Changes in the composition, for example, have altered population structures. For although the majority of the population is rural based, there continue to occur small but significant shifts in the distribution and composition of populations through migration. These trends suggest changes in social processes and in the total scale of societal activity.

How are women entrepreneurs affected by the various processes of change and conflict? What are the qualitative and quantitative manifestations of such processes as migration, urbanization, industrialization, indigenization or Africanisation?

It has been argued that colonialism had a significant impact upon the role of African women as a whole. However, as new forms of structural dependence emerge, such as the investment of multinational corporations, in the internal markets of Africa, what might be the consequences for small scale entrepreneurs? Some observers contend that market women are in danger of being pushed out of the market by big commercial enterprises. (6)

The Zimbabwe government is advancing new policies for development which will have a profound effect on the future of entrepreneurship. Some economies, with the view of fostering a more equitable distribution of goods and services, have become more institutionalized through emerging public corporations or parastatals. Attempts are being made to change internal distribution and transportation systems as well as to impose less restrictive licensing, import, and price controls. But still, the future of the women does not look very bright.

Women in Harare do not appear to occupy a recognized place in the marketing activities of the city. Hawker's licenses issued by the City Council of Harare are issued to men more than women. Women account for a much larger percentage of prosecutions for illegal hawking than men.

Credit

Lack of access to credit both formal and informal is another major barrier often restricting women's ability to smooth consumption over time and to undertake productive activities. Evidence from Cote d'Ivoire and Kenya suggests that women have a lower likelihood of borrowing from formal sources and even from other individuals because of collateral, social and cultural barriers, and the nature of women's businesses. (7)

Property that is acceptable as collateral, especially land, is usually in men's names, and the valuables women own such as jewelry are often deemed unacceptable by formal financial institutions.(8) The transaction costs in obtaining credit for transport, paper work, time spent waiting and so on may be higher for women because of higher opportunity costs from forgone activities.

Women's lower education levels, coupled with social and cultural barriers, constrain their mobility and their interaction with predominantly male credit officers. Seclusion, illiteracy, and lack of title to land or other assets reduce women's access to formal credit. Heavy responsibilities for care and provisioning in the household restrict women's working hours and mobility in ways that affect their choice of sector and of business practices. (9)

Women's businesses thus tend to be smaller and grow slower than men's. They are likely to be home based and to be in sectors that are technologically unsophisticated and overcrowded to the point of market saturation. These business characteristics mean that women entrepreneurs are perceived as poor credit risks.

Legal and Regulatory Barriers

Legal and regulatory barriers prevent women in some countries form fully participating in formal labor markets. (10) For example, legal restrictions that forbid women to enter contracts in their own name may bar women from some lines of work. A study of six countries in the Middle East; Egypt, Jordan, Kuwait, Morocco, Turkey and Tunisia, found that labor laws forbade women to engage in night work and dangerous work (11), though the definitions and categories vary across the countries.

Even in some transitional economies, labor laws prohibit women's employment in certain occupations. (12) Such laws may have been instituted to protect women workers, reflecting the existing cultural norms, but in practice they may actually reduce women's participation.

Western colonization modified these indigenous customs by introducing private ownership and individual registration of land, often discriminating against women. Furthermore, since women usually obtained land rights through a male relative, there was no guarantee that they would retain the rights after a husband's death or divorce.(13)

The absence of formal land rights and the smaller plots of land cultivated by women are critical since land is usually needed as collateral in credit markets.(14) The ability of women to exercise the full range of land rights, to sell or mortgage the land, is essential to the equitable functioning of land markets. (15)

Providing Financial Services to Women

High transactional costs, high perceived risks of default, a lack of collateral and social resistance, commonly bar women access to credit. One way to reduce transaction costs is group lending, in which members accept joint liability for loans. This relieves the lender of the costly process of checking the credit worthiness of individual borrowers and lowers the administrative costs per loan, which is particularly important if the average loan is very small. Group lending also spares borrowers elaborate application procedures, transportation costs, and the need for collateral. Other techniques for lowering transaction costs include inexpensive and mobile offices, hiring of staff from client communities, and standardized and decentralized procedures for lending. Group lending also lowers the risk of default. The combination of peer pressure and co-operative gains from participation in a group has proved to be an effective motivator or for repayment in many different countries and settings world wide. (16)

The risk of default to the overall viability of the lending institution is also minimized by the common practice of making small, short term loans and by rewarding good repayment performance with repeat loans of escalating value. The average loan size could be under Z$100.

Viable Lending to Poor Entrepreneurs

1. Offer Short loan terms, compatible with enterprise outlay and income pattern.
2. Offer repeat loans; full repayment of one loan brings access to another. Repeating lending allows credit to support financial management as a process, not an isolated event.
3. Allow relatively unrestricted use of loans. While most programs select customers with active enterprises (and thus cash flow for repayment) there are few limitations on the uses of loans. Thus, clients have decision making flexibility to use funds for household or enterprise purposes.
4. Extend very small loans, appropriate for meeting the day to day financial requirements of women's businesses. Average loan sizes should be well under Z$100.
5. Make operations customer friendly. Offer low client transaction costs, establish local outlets close to entrepreneurs, and use extremely simple applications (often one page). Limit time between application

and disbursement to a few days and develop a public image of being approachable by the poor people.

Credit Loans for the Women

There is now a large array of literature on how poor women in developing countries make a living, particularly in the informal sector. However, there is strong disagreement as to how to define these women's livelihoods. One thing that has become less obscure is the fact that poor women are in need of working capital to initiate and continue with their income generating activity. (Call this micro-enterprise, petty commodity production, self employment, or whatever.) (17)

Even if their activity provides the main source of (household) income, women often find it extremely difficult to obtain access to feasible amounts of money for working capital. There are several reasons for this, including (household) circumstances of poverty, hierarchical power and gender relationships within the family, societal interpretation of the worth of women, economic activities, and so on. There are a number of studies (Abbot 1993; 119-22, Savava 1987, 61, Tinker 1985:13) backing the suggestion that men carry out more lucrative activities within the informal sector simply because their large share of working capital allows them to do so. (18) Women on the other hand, have to constantly borrow daily amounts form relatives, friends, and money lenders, in order to continue with their crucial but undermined income generating activities.

The recognition of this fact has led both academics and development planners to furiously debate interventionist strategies of providing "credit injections for women from within formal financial systems." However, banks have not always responded positively. Bank managers, used to dealing with large transactions, do not consider it worth the administrative annoyance that is involved in lending and recovering the smaller, weaker section loans. Often, the transaction cost to the bank is greater than the amount lent. Furthermore, the borrowers do not fit with the conventional image of business lending. Weaker section borrowers are often illiterate, and sometimes have no fixed abode or proof of family income and self employment.

The banks half hearted attitude to weaker section lending programs is reflected by the minimal level of resources allocated to these programs by some branches. The clients themselves are fearful of bureaucracy and officialdom and are often frightened by the implications of non-payment. Altogether this adds up to reluctance on behalf of the clients to borrow and the banks to lend.

Recommendation—Summary

The government of Zimbabwe must promote and support women's self-employment and the development of small enterprises and strengthen women's access to credit and capital on appropriate terms equal to those of men through the scaling up of institutions dedicated to promoting women's entrepreneurship, including as appropriate, non-traditional and mutual credit schemes, as well as innovative linkages with financial institutions. Enhance at the national and local levels, rural women's income generating potential by facilitating their equal access to and control over productive resources, land, credit, capital, property rights development programs, and co-operative structures. Strengthen micro-enterprises, new small businesses, co-operative enterprises, expanded markets, and other employment opportunities, and where appropriate facilitate the transition from the informal to the formal sector, especially in rural areas. Establish appropriate mechanisms and encourage inter-sect oral institutions that enable women's co-operatives to optimize access to necessary services. Increase the proportion of women extension workers and other government personnel who provide technical assistance or administer economic programs. Review and implement policies, including business, commercial, and contract law and government regulations to ensure that they do not discriminate against micro, small, and medium scale enterprises owned by women in rural and urban areas. Co-ordinate and implement policies that integrate the needs and interests of employed, self employed, and entrepreneurial women, into sect oral and inter-ministerial policies, programs, and budgets. Increase the participation of women, including women entrepreneurs from all sectors and their organizations, to contribute to the formulation and review of policies and programs being developed by economic ministries and banking institutions. Mobilize the banking sector to increase lending and refinancing through incentives and the development of intermediaries that serve the needs of women entrepreneurs and producers in both rural and urban areas and include women in their leadership, planning, and decision making. Structure services to reach rural and urban women involved in micro, small and medium scale enterprises, with special attention to young women, low income women, and indigenous women who lack access to capital and assets. Expand women's access to financial markets by identifying and encouraging financial, supervisory, and regulatory reforms that support financial institutions' direct and indirect efforts to better meet the credit and other financial needs of the micro, small and medium scale enterprises of women. Promote greater involvement of women beneficiaries at the project planning and implementation stages to ensure access to jobs and contracts.

Non-governmental organizations in Zimbabwe have a role to play in the economic empowerment of Zimbabwean women. Many organizations are imaging in erratic progression, but they are doing very little about the economic empowerment of women. These institutions are required to pay special attention to women's needs when disseminating market, trade, and resource information and provide appropriate training in these fields. Develop flexible funding arrangements to finance intermediary institutions that target women's economic activities and promote self sufficiency and increased capacity in and profitability of women's economic enterprises. Develop programs that provide training and retraining, particularly in new technologies and affordable services to women in business management, product development, financing, production and quality control, marketing, and the legal aspects of business. Provide outreach programs to inform low income and poor women, particularly in rural and remote areas, of opportunities for market and technology access, and provide assistance taking advantage of such opportunities. Disseminate information about successful women entrepreneurs in both traditional and non-traditional economic activities and the skills necessary to achieve success, and facilitate networking and the exchange of information.

To have the full participation of women in the business sector, organizations should support the economic activities of indigenous women, taking into account their traditional knowledge so as to improve their situation and development. The financial intermediaries, national training institutes, credit unions, non-governmental organisations, women's association, professional organizations, and the private sector should provide at the national and regional levels, training in a variety of business related, financial, management, and technical skills, to enable women, especially young women, to participate in economic policy making at those levels. Provide business services including: marketing and trade information, product design and innovation, and technology transfer and quality, to women's business enterprises, including those in the export sector of the economy. Invest capital and develop investment portfolios to finance women's business enterprises. Support credit networks and innovative ventures including traditional savings schemes. Provide networking arrangements for entrepreneurial women including opportunity for the mentoring of inexperienced women by the more experienced.

Women business Organizations in Zimbabwe

The general outcry by most African women when it comes to their socio-economic marginalization has prompted Zimbabwean women to do something practical about rectifying the situation.

Their solution is entrepreneurship, which has long been recognised as a key factor in the economic empowerment of women. Business in Zimbabwe is regarded as a male domain, regardless of evidence that 70% of small businesses are owned by women.

Women who venture into the business world encounter worse problems than men. For instance, fewer women obtain business loans than men. Also, women are victims of systematic prejudice (discriminatory laws, policies, financial constrains) and years of neglect (socio-culturally, educationally, and legislatively) as regards business. To combat this problem, women have launched the Oma Bank Capital Account Project (Oma stands for Omana/madzimai, meaning "women"). This implies that the project is strictly for women, and is aimed at economically empowering women, even though men are allowed (mainly as clients) into the project.

The idea of a women's bank was first put forward in 1982 by the Ministry of Community Development and Women's Affairs, as a means by which rural women could get access to credit facilities. Although the idea received resounding support from women, it did not immediately get off the ground because of financial constraints. The International Conference on Employment Creation, held in 1993, also recommended a women's bank to provide access to credit for the majority of the unemployed, who are women.

According to Thenjiwe Lesabe, Zimbabwe's Minister of National Affairs, Employment and Co-operatives (in which the Department of Women's Affairs falls), this idea came after the realization that many women were embarking on micro enterprises as a cushioning measure against rising inflation and unemployment, brought about by the results of the economic reform program.

Women found it difficult to get money from financial institutions. The National report prepared for the Beijing Conference on Women, held in China in September 1995, also identified priority areas of concern, and one of them was the micro enterprise credit facility. It was clear that there was a need for a women's bank.

The Oma Bank

"The Oma Bank Capital Account Project is open to all women throughout the country, but they can only buy shares through a women's organization and not as individuals. Members are required to deposit $70 a month, or $840 a year, in the Oma Capital Account with the Post Office Savings Bank (P.O.S.B.), until the Oma Bank is fully set up. The money will earn tax free interest of 16% from the P.O.S.B. and the rate will remain fixed for the next 12 months. After 12 months, the period by which it is expected sufficient funds will have been accumulated to set up the bank, the capital contributions will be transferred to the Oma Bank, and the women will receive shares in it," said Ms. Gloria Ndoro Mukombachoto, the Oma Bank Project's consultant. "The P.S.O.B. is ideal because it has the largest branch network in the country, consisting of more than 200 Post Offices and banking halls," she added.

The Oma Federation

The Oma Federation is a consortium of 13 non-governmental organizations whose membership consists mainly of women. The Federation was formed in July 1996, as a means of showing commitment and participation in all events, leading up to the launch of the Oma Project with P.O.S.B. Although the current membership of the federation is 13 organizations, it is open to other women's organizations. To ensure that the project is a success, Oma Project has put together a technical committee, comprised of highly qualified women from various professional fields whose duties and responsibilities include:

- Acting as an advisory group to the Oma Federation.
- Developing the Oma Bank's "Comprehensive Development Program."
- Identifying and determining the Bank's future infrastructure, (human, financial and others).
- Develop the Oma Bank's input and output activities. This is done with the assistance of the Oma Federation and all other share holders.(19)

Unity of Purpose

Oma Federation members have unity of purpose. Their target is to raise $50 million in order to set up a development commercial bank that will, among other things, bring banking to the marginalized groups in Zimbabwe, The fact that at least 60% of share holdings will be set aside, to be taken up by women through the various women's organizations, demonstrates that sustainable development can never be given to people. It must come from the people themselves.

The Zimbabwe Women's Bureau
(Z.W.B.)

The Zimbabwe Women's Bureau helps women in rural areas to fulfill their defined role in the area of food production and resources management. Z.W.B. is a non-governmental member of the Natural Farming Network (N.F.N.), a coalition of 10 national N.G.O.'s and government agencies that promotes improved agricultural practices and natural resource management. The work of Z.W.B. is an example of how the network relates to its members and supports the extension needs of women. Z.W.B. functions through 13 field workers in 13 different districts. Z.W.B. focuses on skills training related to community group projects. Each field worker works with 10 to 12 community groups. Each group defines its goals with respect to literacy, skills training, gender awareness, credit and project management, and natural resources management. About half of the projects assisted by Z.W.B. are agricultural.

One Million Dollar Credit Club

This type of credit institution was formed by Harare North Member of Parliament, Nyasha Chikwinya, in 1996. Women members contribute $100 a month. Member ship is not limited and is open to all women.

Thrift and Savings

The co-operative thrift and savings have been very difficult to establish in Zimbabwe due to spending habits. The thrift and credit societies are created to serve the interests of the farmers and petty traders. The Hawkers and Vendors Association of Zimbabwe (H.A.V.A.Z.) established a similar savings but it is headed by men. Women and men members contribute to the society according to what the poorest member can afford to pay.

There is also the lending of money to farmers by brokers and money lenders, who charge the farmers very high interest rates because there is no bank co-operation. Money lenders in general are not desirable sources of credit, since the rate of interest charged is so high. The lenders and brokers enjoy a financial advantage at the expense of the farmers and market women. They argue that the high interest charged is due to the fact that most of the traders are great risks. They further feel that due to the uncertainty in agriculture, the lenders may not be sure of being paid at harvest time.

Improvements of the level of living and increasing productivity are not only acceptable social objectives in Zimbabwe, but are economic necessities as well. The improvement of women's programs over both long and short term will give women a position of decision making, although in most of the co-operative groups studied, women seemed to have the least membership.

Young Women's Christian Association (Y.W.C.A.)

It is world affiliated to the world Y.W.C.A with headquarters in Geneva. It was established in 1957. It has individual members of more than 3000 in Zimbabwe.

Activities

The Association runs education programs among the youth and women in the areas of leadership, health youth work project management and rural development.

National Federation of Business and Professional Women of Zimbabwe-Mutare

It is affiliated to the International Federation of Business and Professional women. It has individual members up to 500. It was established in 1949.

Activities

Promote professional and business women, education and employment conditions, health, legislation, U.N.E.S.C.O., and status of women.

Zimbabwe Association of University Women

Affiliated with International Federation of University Women. It has 200 individual members. It was established in 1956.

Activities

Education and status of women, scholarship award to African girls, cultural meetings.

Women in Business

This organization was formed in 1990 by its President, Violet Madzimbamuto. Membership is not limited and is open to all women.

Activities

Specializes in skills training for the business women in Zimbabwe, in order to help them face the challenges of the business community.

Citations

1. Christine Obbo, African Women, *Their Struggle for Economic Independence 1980.*
2. Women and Development in Africa. Comparative Perspective. Edited by Jane L. Parpart. Dalhousie African Studies series 7.
3. Enhancing Women's Participation in Economic Development p.cm—(A World Bank policy paper) HQ 1240. E37.1994.
4. Christine Obbo, African Women, *Their Struggle for Economic Independence 1980.*
5. Njoku, John E. Eberegbulam *The world of the African Women* copyright 1980 by John E. Eberegbulam Njoku in the United States of America.
6. Maria Rosa, Women of Africa, *Roots of Oppression* by Faro Buonoparte 52, 20121 Milan—first published in English in an updated edition by Zed Press, 57. Caledonian Rd, London NI.9 DN 1983.
7. Enhancing Women's Participation in Economic Development p. cm—(A World Bank policy paper HQ 1240 E37 1994 p.184.
8. Bringing Women in Women's Issues in International Development Programs by Niiket Kardam HQ 1240 K 371990.
9. Enhancing Women's Participation in Economic Development p. cm—(A World Bank policy paper) HQ 1240. E 37 1994 p.184.
10. Women, Work, and Gender Relations in Developing Countries—A Global Perspective. Edited by Parvin Ghorayshi and Claire Belanger. HQ1240 W 6659 1996.
11. Women Work and Gender.
12. Women Work and Gender.
13. Rural Development and Women in Africa. International Labor Office, Geneva HQ 1240. 5. A35 R87 1986.
14. Women Work and Gender.
15. Rural Development and Women in Africa. International Labor Office, Geneva HQ 1240. 5. A 35 R87 1986.
16. Enhancing Women's Participation in Economic Development p. cm—(A World Bank policy paper) HQ 1240. E 37 1994.

17. Women, Work, and Gender Relations in Developing Countries—A Global Perspective. Edited by Parvin Ghorayshi and Claire Belanger. HQ1240 W 6659 1996. p.184.

18. Women Work and Gender p. 184.

19. OMA BANK http://www.freeworld,it/peacelink/anb-bia/nr319/eo4.html.

Chapter 7

Women and Politics in Zimbabwe

Whatever the nature of the state and politics, women are almost never central to it. In Western democracies, where women enjoy formal equality with men and their participation on voting is equal to men, there has with the major exception of Nordic countries, been a marked consistency in the low figures for female participation in national policy-making, ranging between two and ten percent.(1) Comparable figures for sub-Saharan Africa indicate that in 1987 on average only six percent of the members of national legislatures were women. In ministerial positions they reached, in no country, more than four women ministers. Over half of all countries had no women ministers at all.(2) In Africa, as elsewhere, democracy has proven to be no guarantee for a more equal representation of women in government, there are alarming indications that representation has in some cases declined. Despite the glaring of under-representation of women in political decision-making, western feminism through the 1960's and 1970's did not place much emphasis on getting women into the formal politics of political parties, parliaments, or national assemblies, but registered skepticism towards these orthodox channel's of representation.

Until recently African women too, have largely withdrawn from politics, preferring instead to manage what is left of their affairs autonomously. (3) But opting out of politics is not necessarily due to political apathy, as some men would like us to believe. Rather it is on the experience that women enter politics on terms set by the male elite who use women's political energy for their own ends.(4) In much of Africa the terms imposed by the male elite are particularly restrictive. Women's role in politics is often understood to be limited to a particular female space, such as a party's women's wing, where its members are given little or no scope to influence policy formulation, not even policies that are directly relevant to them.

Older and less educated to them might content themselves with the role of submissive but ardent party supporter, but young professional women fell alienated by the dancing, and ululating women who praise the virtues of dependent wifehood and dismiss independent women as "prostitutes." Lacking other alternatives, professional African women have instead retreated with their grievances into the non-governmental organizations (NGO) sector where women's groups and funding from international donors abound.

The discourse of the NGO sector has been dominated by the women in development (WID) debate which has remained divorced from economic and political empowerment goals(5), at best emphasizing self-help, consciousness-raising, and research on discriminatory laws and practices, at worst stressing social welfare aspects. It is only recently that the women's NGO sector has in a number of places assumed a more explicitly political character and that professional women have called for more equitable political representation and empowerment. Despite such advocacy, the majority of NGO women have remained opposed to involving themselves in party politics, and the division that existed between political and civic women has continued even if the women politicians have emerged from the NGO's. This raises questions about the efficiency of increasing the political representation of women as a way of increasing influence on policy formulation, and about the nature of the representation of women's interests as such.

This chapter focuses on the limitations women politicians experience in the male domain of party politics and government and examines the nature and the reasons for division between women politicians and members of the women's movement. It tries above all to explain why the disproportion between those elected and those who elect is too astounding to be attributed to accident.(6)

In Zimbabwe women entered politics with the promise of gender equality. The armed independence struggle, which led to the democratically elected government of the Zimbabwe African National Union (ZANU) in 1980, had been long and protracted. By 1979 the Zimbabwe African National Liberation Army (ZANLA), the armed wing of ZANU, had recruited over 10,000 trained women guerrilla fighters and a number of those had been appointed to high command.(7)

Initially, the involvement of women as combatants was resisted because, like elsewhere in Africa, women were perceived to be situated in the private sphere, and their role was defined as offering support services for the male fighters. It was both the insistence of women and the need for more combatants that brought about a change of attitude in the male for more combatants that brought about a change of attitude in the male leadership. Opening the first ZANU (PF) Women's League Conference in 1984, President Robert Mugabe admitted that the original view of the party shown during the first years following its ban was to recruit only male cadres for military training and female cadres for academic and secretarial courses. The belief we then had, which obviously was a mistaken belief, was that only male cadres could prosecute an armed struggle.(8) From 1972 onwards, women joined the armed struggle, first as carriers of military equipment and later as front-line fighters. In 1977 a Department of Women's Affairs of the party, the forerunner to the ZANU (PF) Women's League, was formed and two years later held its first conference in Mozambique. There, its functions were defined as political, military, and diplomatic, and President Robert Mugabe reaffirmed that "by waging the armed struggle, the party had created therefore, a process generation of forces that will result in the total liberation of the women."(9)

As combatants many women experienced equality with men for the first time, and experienced both the exhilarating and the problematic. Oppah Rushesha, Deputy Minister of Environment in 1994, who joined ZANLA at age seventeen and was promoted to commander, explains the dilemma of sudden elevation from minority to majority status: "We did not have the age of majority then, women were second class citizens. So being independent for the first time, you had to take decisions that really affected you own life without having to consult your parents or some other superior. So in that it was important for women to understand that they must behave like they are equals of their male counterparts."

For Margaret Dongo, a former ZANU PF Member of Parliament and an ex-combatant, "the war was the beginning of women's struggles for equality. Gender differences were suspended in the camps, men and women cooked, fought and trained together, irrespective of their gender. Male fighters assured women of equality after independence, and many of the young women who joined the army towards the end of the war consider their combatant years, despite the hardships it involved, as having been great fun."(10)

For many other women, particularly in the rural areas, who supported the guerrillas with running errands, cooking, washing, and supplying sexual services on demand and at times under duress, the struggle did not offer fundamentally new gender roles. (11) Nonetheless, both combatants and auxiliary women in different ways became aware of their subordination to men, or at least their own abilities to make decisions and take action. Some rural women for example, used the change of gender-ideologies that took place during the war to renegotiate relationships within the household. (12) Many of the women ex-combatants felt rejected by post-war society that had reverted to old value systems. Because women had lived side by side with men, they were now labeled "loose" women, and parents would not allow their sons to marry an ex-combatant, thinking they would not make good wives. In real life the virtues of being an independent woman were again undesirable to parents, to men, and it seemed, to the new government.

Against expectations and hopes, very few women were brought into the new government. During the first term of office between 1980-1985, only 11 out of a total of 150 parliamentarians were women, and in the 1981 district council elections women made up 22 of a total of 1182 councilors. (13) By 1994 the number of women councilors had further dropped to five nationally. The mandate of the ZANU PF Women's League had swiftly moved from military objectives to social welfare and party mobilization, adjunctive to the main party, because actually they have transferred the role of the kitchen to the Women's League. (14)

Photographs of the 1984 conference of the ZANU PF Women's League show row upon row of elderly women, clad in party colors with the face of their president prominently displayed on their garments. As elsewhere women were important as voters only and they had been limited to party membership, attending rallies and other meetings, providing labor and entertainment at such gatherings, and being mobilized for demonstration and activities. (15)

The Rise and fall of the Ministry of Women's Affairs in Zimbabwe

Under pressure to initiate the total liberation of women, promised during the liberation struggle, the ZANU PF government established the Ministry in 1981, appointing the secretary of the ZANU PF Women's League, Teurai Ropa Nhongo, an ex-combatant who had long been a member of the central committee of the party as its head. The role of the Ministry was described as an instrument that articulates women's demands and initiates and administers development programs for women and communities. The activities of the ministry evolved around a project approach that stressed adult literacy, the establishment of pre-schools, and income generating projects such as sewing, knitting, handicrafts, and poultry production. (16) Critics at the time charged that the women were going on with their piecemeal, isolated, project approach as if they were a separate nation within the national development plan. (17) The ministry was indeed considered marginal to national development and was allocated a correspondingly small budget, which in 1984 barely covered the salaries of the ministry's staff. (18)

More effective, perhaps was the legal department of the ministry, which initiated a number of ambitious law reforms. Most important were the 1982 Legal Age of Majority Act which conferred on women legal majority status at the age of 18, and the Matrimonial Causes act of 1985, which equalized the divorce law and acknowledged a wife's contribution to the marital property. The Department of Women's Affairs at that time attracted a number of professional women who were well qualified to the gender debate but also to push for legal changes affecting their own status as professional women. Unlike their more uneducated sisters, who have either remained uninformed about the laws or excluded by customary marriage, they might have been the main beneficiaries of the new legislation, but they distanced themselves from the ministry before long.

Part of the problem was the close relationship the ministry had to the party and the Women's League therein, its minister representing both. This was not surprising since ZANU PF envisioned the supremacy of the party over the government. "The party," declared President Mugabe in 1884, "is the creator of policy which government implements."(19) Effectually this also meant that the party determined the policy direction of the Ministry of Community Development and Women's Affairs. Its head lamented in 1984 that because the ministry did not administer any statute, it had no mandate to introduce laws in Parliament, neither can it amend any. All we can do is to make recommendations for change to the appropriate ministries who usually take their time to respond.(20) The relative powerlessness of the ministry vis-à-vis the party and the government became painfully clear one year later when the government authorized the rounding-up of unaccompanied women under the pretext that they were prostitutes or vagrants, during "Operation Clean-Up," which targeted mainly young single women, squatters and vagrants.

Thousands of women over the whole country were detained under the vagrancy act. Those who could not produce marriage certificates were sent to a resettlement area in the Zambezi Valley, deprived of courts and lawyers. (21) Far from being prostitutes, many of the affected women felt targeted, because they were young, single, and showed evidence of earning their own living. The operation was interpreted as an attempt to control women who had become too independent.(22) Contravening the basic human right to the freedom of movement, it effectively reversed the Legal Age of Majority for those women who were making use of the law by evidently digressing from their traditional role as dependent wives.

The Department of Women's Affairs claimed that it had neither been informed nor consulted over the matter, and although its minister was heard to say critical words about the incident, it apparently never publicly condemned "Operation Clean-Up," declaring that it would be improper to criticize a government of which it was part and parcel.(23) Moreover, the ministry was unable to stop subsequent round-ups. Professional women who had been, they felt, the main target distanced themselves from the Ministry of Women's Affairs. As a direct result, the Women's Action Group was formed. Its purpose was to document and protest against the rounding-up of women and to campaign for the release of those detained.(24) The group was denounced as expatriate dominated, as lacking in aims and objectives, and as having antagonized the women's organization with the strongest grassroots support in the country, namely the ZANU PF Women's League. (25) Similar women's groups nonetheless emerged from 1984 onwards.

Possibly in reaction Women's Affairs proposed in 1985, was the formation of a National Women's Council, who's predominately government, appointed members were to act as an umbrella organization for all women NGOs. It was organized in a structure parallel to the Women's League from village to national level, and under the auspices of the Ministry of Women's Affairs. Its tasks were to include acting as a clearing house for all external funding and to ensure that programs and actions were in harmony with government aspirations and ambitions. Commenting on the proposed relationship between the Women's League and the Council, Teurai Ropa Nhongo explained, "As a nation which is moving towards a one party state, I must emphasize on the supremacy of the Women's League. The Women's League is the policy maker that gives direction to women's activities and the National Women's Council is its implementer. The National Women's Council translates the policy directions provided by the Women's League into Action."(26)

The council would have effectively curtailed the independence of the NGO women and brought them under control of the party, something independent women and the foreign donors that support them have thus far successfully resisted. The Department of Women's Affairs, however, was moved even closer to the party, so that its functions now overlap with the women's league. In 1989 the department was integrated on a smaller scale into the newly established Ministry of Political Affairs, physically housed in the ZANU PF headquarters. It was mandated to service the Women's League. Teurai Ropa Mujuru lost her position as minister, and at the conference of the ZANU PF Women's league that year she also lost the leadership of that organization to the late wife of the President, Sally Mugabe, who together with the rest or the league leadership, was unexpectedly appointed by her husband. (27)

After the change, independent women asked if Women's Affairs had now become a party function and not a government body. Or is it a form of check and balance to curb the newly emerging power of women in the political arena? (28)

In the new ministry, staff was reduced and former sections transferred to other ministries. "Most of the people we had in the old ministry left. A lot of them are now in the private sector running NGO's," bemoans Bridgit Mugabe, a sister of the president and the co-coordinator of Women Affairs. In 1992 the department was moved again to the Ministry of National Affairs also housed with ZANU PF headquarters. The department was reduced to just the co-coordinator.(29) It no longer has a proper link with the government, since the secretary of the Women's League is a minister of Women's Affairs without cabinet portfolio.

The contraction and gradual merging of the national machinery with the party structures has signaled for the NGO women that they have lost all possibility of directly influencing government, and they see their role restricted to advocacy. They have certainly not been encouraged to join the party and they have learned to expect nothing positive from the national machinery. Ultimately it means that if one is not in the party, one is not represented. So if women are to be politically heard it will have to be through the Women's League. Or one can presuppose that by not being in the league one has automatically alienated oneself from any meaningful input into policy formulation and the political process. (30) For the majority of professional women this problem still seems to hold.

In both Botswana and Zambia educated women have never had much share in post independence political participation, and they had not sought it. Unlike in Zimbabwe, they are only now demanding such representation. The change of heart was triggered by two events, the move from one-party rule to multi-party democracy in 1991 in Zambia and the unconfirmed rumor in Botswana in 1993, that the government was considering holding a referendum with a view to secure people's agreement to have the Botswana constitution changed to entrench gender based discrimination. In both cases non-governmental women's organizations were moved to question and reverse their rejection of formal politics.

As a consequence, women NGO alliances and lobby groups, while still keeping aloof from party affiliations and ostensibly not seeking political office for their own members, set themselves the task to get more women onto government.

In Zimbabwe, women constitute the majority of voters, but they do not vote for each other if they can help it. While many agree that women are discriminated against, they lay the blame for their under-representation in politics at the feet of other women.

Men can be fought, defied, begged, accommodated, dealt with in manners used in the private sphere;, other women remain an unknown. Defining their problems, women politicians and women activists stress the lack of support of other women as the greatest obstacle of all. The division between women appears to be deep and many-layered. Women politicians among themselves are said not to support each other. NGO women are said to not support their sisters in politics, women in politics are accused of not supporting the cause of the women's movements, educated women seem to dislike the less fortunate, and vice versa. There are divisions that cut across, sell-outs, queen bees, and elitists, compete with the very gender sensitive and the merely gender aware and the gender ignorant.

In the cacophony of allegations and counter-allegations, one truth shines through; the realization that the diversionist discourse is not always, but often, a reflection of the attitudes and prejudices men have about women, and that divisions are the result of discrimination rather that its cause. In a situation where the number of positions available to women is kept limited, there is fierce competition and mistrust. Scarcity of opportunity also limits the scope of action for those wishing to be considered, precisely because politics are male dominated, and because merit, suitability and with it, the benefit of promotion are defined strictly in accordance with patriarchal interests and ambitions. Lack of opportunities for promotion breeds petty jealousies and the rumors they feed on, At times they are started or instigated by a virulent press, or fellow male politicians. If for example one women deputy minister resigns after another women is appointed her superior, the resignation must be the outcome of jealousy and the fact that even women cannot tolerate a women as a boss. Women politicians who bemoan the fact that they get no support and those petty jealousies play in to the hands of men; contribute themselves to the divisive discourse. At the most basic of levels the suggestion that women in mainstream politics, because they operate in a male dominated environment, must be sexually immoral, casts its shadows.

Fellow women in the party and ordinary citizens know that women are seldom appointed on merit, so they must have rubbed the right shoulders, or worse still, slept their way up, particularly if they do not fall into the obvious mute party supporter category.

If women appointees are not thought to have granted sexual favors, they must have been appointed because they are submissive, not very sharp, or otherwise weak, a suggestion that is based on some experience within the women's wings of parties.

There is little doubt that some women are indeed favored and appointed on account of the fact that they represent male ideals of womanhood, which does not question male superiority.

In Zambia and Zimbabwe young professional women have also been appointed and elected into government and these women, while they distance themselves from the obviously co-opted, are themselves not immune to accusations of having sold out, not so much by fellow politicians but by the women's movement.

Women in politics are not just party members, but they are most of all women who have to fulfill a specific set of criteria if they wish to merit promotion. What constitutes merit for women is decided by the party leadership, reflecting and reinforcing male informed notions of women's inferior and dependent status. And the limits of merit are even more restrictive if competition for political office is stiff. The electoral systems considered here are of the first past the post single member constituency type, which the world over are notorious for being particularly unfavorable to women, because men tend to be very protective of the few opportunities they have for entering legislation and high political office.(31)

A different yet just as gender specific set of expectations is applied to women politicians by the women's movement whose notion of merit is defined by gender sensitivity and the willingness and ability to oppose the value systems that parties impose on their women members. They envision women in politics to have a special mission beyond party lines. Underlying this is the nagging question whether women will change institutions before institutions change women. (32)

For the women's movement this dilemma is particularly pronounced. The realization recently that in order to overcome the inefficiency of advocacy from outside the political institutions they have to seek access to their structures, goes hand in hand with a deep mistrust of both the structures and the women who are prepared to work within their structures.

Women's wings are not particular to Africa, but they have been particularly pervasive in reinforcing public/private as male/female dichotomies. The history of the ZANU PF Women's League which had moved form military command structures to being a "kitchen" in less that a decade and in a nominally democratic political system, suggests that there is little tangible hope that separate women's party structures could be transformed into arenas to effectively push for gender equality in the near future. It is because of these structures that intellectual women have rejected formal politics as avenue for change, and that women politicians even when they act independently of the women's wing, have remained suspicious to the women's movement. It is the dissatisfaction with the limitations of party politics that conditions the women's movement to largely ignore parties, not only in that they personally abhor the thought of getting involved, but also in their strategies.

After the very contentious 1995 elections the new Zimbabwean parliament housed the largest number of women's MP's since independence and has attracted to politics a new crop of professionals and ex-combatant women. They gained support of a more mature electorate disillusioned with a male party elite that had showed little concern for their voters.(33) It might well be that the new South African government, which due mainly to the quota system adopted by the African National Congress (ANC), brought 106 women into parliament and moved the country from being one of the most conservative to one of the most progressive in terms of representation of women in government, (34) has inspired women voters and even some male politicians in the region.

Recommendation and Summary

The government should protect and promote the equal rights of women to engage in political activities and to freedom of association, including membership in political parties and trade unions. It should review the different impact of electoral systems on the political representations of women in elected bodies and consider where appropriate, the adjustment or reform of these systems. All political parties in Zimbabwe should consider examining party structures and procedures to remove all barriers that directly or indirectly discriminate against the participation of women. The government should encourage a vertical structure, as described from the Ugandan experience, for constant communication among women politicians and women voters at all levels of government.(35) A horizontal structure, or world-wide caucus of women parliamentarians using electronic communication strategies such as Feminist Majority On-line, the world-wide web-site of the Feminist Majority.(36) Exchange visits between groups of women politicians from different countries that would serve as political education and information sharing. Change campaign financing laws and create public financing for candidates that would facilitate women candidates.

Citations

1. Anne Phillips, Engendering Democracy (Press, Cambridge, 1991) p.62.
2. United Nations, World's Women. Trends and Statistics 1970-1990 (United nations New York, 1991) pp 32, 39, 40.
3. Kathleen Staudt, "Women's Politics, the State, and Capitalist Transformation in Africa," in Irving L. Markovitz (ed.), Studies in Power and Class in Africa (Oxford University, New York, 1987) p.207.
4. Kathleen Staudt, "Stratification. Implication for Women's Politics'" in Claire Robertson and Iris Berger (eds.), Women and Class in Africa (Africana, New York 1986), p201.
5. Maria Nzomo, "Engineering Democratization in Kenya, A political perspective, in Wanjiku M. Kabira, Jacquenline A. Odoul and Maria Nzomo (eds.), Democratic Change in Africa. Women's Perspective (AAWORD, Nairobi, 1993), p13.
6. Phillip, Engendering Democracy, p.77.
7. Ruvimbo Chimedza "Integration of Women in Development with Particular Reference to Zimbabwe," in selected papers and proceedings of a workshop organized by the ILO, SWAPO, and UNIN, Lusaka, Zambia, 5-15 October 1983 (ILO, Geneva, 1985), p97.
8. ZANU (PF), "Opening Address by the President of ZANU (PF) Comrade R.G. Mugabe, in speeches and documents of the first ZANU (PF) Women's League Conference (ZANU PF), Women's League, (Harare, 1994) p.7.
9. Interviews, Harare, 16 and 18 February 1994.
10. Irene Staunton, Mother of the Revolution (Baobab, Harare, 1990), pp.49 and 81.
11. Rudo Gaidzanwa, "Bourgeois Theories of Gender and Feminism and Their Shortcomings with Reference to Southern African Countries," in Ruth Meena (ed.), Gender in Southern Africa. Conceptual and Theoretical Issues. (SAPES Books, Harare, 1992), p.111.
12. Chimedza, "Integration of Women," p.102.
13. Interview with a woman Member of Parliament, Harare, and 18 February, 1994.

14. Gisela Frese-Weghoft, Frauen Tragen die last (Rowohlt, Reinbeck, Hamburg, 1991), p.176.
15. Chimedza, "Integration of Women," p.102.
16. Elinor Batezat and Margaret Mwalo, Women in Zimbabwe (SAPES Books, Harare, 1989), p.62.
17. Olivia Muchena quoted in Batezat and Mwalo, Women in Zimbabwe.
18. Herald Harare, 22 February, 1984.
19. Zanu PF, "Opening Speech," p.9.
20. Minister Joyce Nhongo Mujuru quoted in Herald Harare, 15 November 1984.
21. "Operation Clean-Up," Moro Gweru, December 1993, January 1994.
22. Susie M. Jacobs and Tracy Howard, "Women in Zimbabwe; Stated Policy and State Action," in Haleh Afshar (ed.), Women and Ideology (Macmillan, London, 1987), p.42.
23. Gaidzanwa "Bourgeois Theories of Gender," p.115.
24. Peggy Watson "Spicy Mixture of Fact and Fiction," Sunday Mail, Harare, 18 November, 1984.
25. Nyaradzo Makamure, "Women's Group, the Failings," Sunday Mail, Harare, 11 November, 1984.
26. Ministry of Community Development and Women's Affairs, The National Women's Council. Extracted from the Address by the Honorable Minister of State, Belvedere Teachers College, 25 January, 1986, Harare.
27. Kwanele Ona Jirira, "The Condition of Women, Has it Improved?," SAPEM Harare, April 1990, pp.19-23.
28. Jirira, "The Condition of Women," p.20.
29. Interview, Harare, 11 February, 1994.
30. Kwanele Ona Jirira, "Women in Zimbabwe, Coming Out of Men's Political Shadows," SAPEM Harare, October 1989, p.35.
31. Pippa Norris, "Conclusions, Comparing Legislative Recruitment," in Lovenduski and Norris, Gender and Party Politics, p.313.
32. Phillips, engendering Democracy, p.74.
33. Lovenduski, "Introduction," p.6.
34. Interviews, Harare, July 1995.
35. Sunday Times Johannesburg, 29 April, 1994 (Gisela Geisler).
36. United Nations, Fourth World Conference on Women in Beijing.

References

1. *Agricultural Extension in Zimbabwe* 1991. A group of rural Zimbabwean women defined what it means to be a woman as: worker, organizer, manager, assistant, and nurse for the home, family, community and the Nation

2. Batezat, Elinor and Margaret Mwalo, *Women in Zimbabwe* (SAPES Books, Harare, 1989), p62.

3. Burdett, Marcia M. "The Role of Women in Zambia," *Between Two Worlds* West View Press 1988 p.56 (65.9.B89)

4. Chimedza, Ruvimbo *"Integration of Women in Development with Particular Reference to Zimbabwe,"* in selected papers and proceedings of a workshop organized by the ILO, SWAPO, and UNIN, Lusaka, Zambia, 5-15 October 1983 (ILO, Geneva, 1985), p97.

5. *Enhancing Women's Participation in Economic Development* p. cm (A world Bank policy paper) HQ 1240. E37.1994.

6. Fourth World Conference on Women in Beijing. (4-25 September 1995) and the parallel NGO Forum on Women 1995 (30 August-8 September).

7. Frese-Weghoft, Gisela *Frauen Tragen Die Last* (Rowohlt, Reinbeck, Hamburg, 1991), p.76.

8. Gaidzanwa, Rudo "Bourgeois Theories of Gender and Feminism and Their Shortcomings with Reference to Southern African Countries," in Ruth Meena (ed.), *Gender in Southern Africa. Conceptual and Theoretical Issues.* (SAPES Books, Harare, 1992), p.111.

9. Geisler, Gisela Sunday Times Johannesburg, 29 April, 1994.

10. Gweru, Moro "Operation Clean-Up," December 1993, January 1994.

11. Herald Harare, 22 February, 1984

12. Integration of Women into the Economy, 1985 p.121.

13. Jacobs, Susie M. and Howard, Tracy, "Women in Zimbabwe; Stated Policy and State Action," in Haleh Afshar (ed.), *Women and Ideology* (Macmillan, London, 1987), p.42.

14. Kardam, Niiket *Women's Issues in International Development Programs* HQ1240K 371990.

15. Kwanele, Ona Jirira, *"The Condition of Women, Has it improved?"* SAPEM Harare, April 1990, pp19-23.

16. Kwanele, Ona Jirira, "*Women in Zimbabwe, Coming Out of Men's Political Shadows*," SAPEM Harare 1989, p35.

17. Lovenduski, "Introduction," p.6.

18. Makamure, Nyaradzo "Women's Group, the Failings," Sunday Mail, Harare 11 November, 1984.

19. Ministry of Community Development and Women's Affairs, The National Women's Council. Extracted from the Address by the Honorable Minister of State, Belvedere Teachers College, 25 January, 1986, Harare.

20. Muchena, Olivia quoted in Batezat and Mwalo, *Women in Zimbabwe*

21. Mugabe, Comrade R.G. ZANU (PF), "Opening Address by the President of ZANU (PF) in speeches and documents of the first ZANU (PF) Women's League Conference (ZANU PF), Women's League, (Harare, 1994) p.7.

22. Mujuru, Joyce Nhongo, Minister, quoted in Herald Harare, 15 November 1984.

23. Norris, Pippa "Conclusions, Comparing Legislative Recruitment," in Lovenduski and Norris, *Gender and Party Politics*, p.313.

24. Nzomo, Maria "Engineering Democratization in Kenya, A political perspective, in Wanjiku M. Kabira, Jacquenline A. Odoul and Maria Nzomo (eds.), *Democratic Change in Africa*. Women's Perspective (AAWORD, Nairobi, 1993), p13.

25. Njoku, John E. Eberegbulam *The world of the African Women* copyright 1980 by John E. Eberegbulam Njoku in the United States of America.

26. Obbo, Christine *African Women, Their Struggle for Economic Independence* ZED Press, 57 Caledonian Rd., London 1980.

27. Parpart, Jane L. *Women and Development in Africa. Comparative Perspective*. Dalhousie African Studies series 7.

28. Phillips, Anne *Engendering Democracy* (Press, Cambridge, 1991) p.62.

29. Rosa, Maria *Women of Africa, Roots of Oppression* by Faro Buonoparte 52, 20121 Milan—first published in English in an updated edition by Zed Press, 57. Caledonian Rd, London NI.9 DN 1983.

30. Rural Development and Women in Africa. International Labor Office, Geneva HQ 1240. 5. A35 R87 1986.

31. Sivard, Ruth Leger *Women, a World Survey* 1985 chapter 18.

32. Staudt, Kathleen "Women's Politics, the State, and Capitalist Transformation in Africa," in Irving L. Markovitz (ed.), *Studies*

in Power and Class in Africa (Oxford University, New York, 1987) p.207.

33. Staudt, Kathleen "Stratification. Implication for Women's Politics'" in Claire Robertson and Iris Berger (eds.), *Women and Class in Africa* (Africana, New York 1986), p201.

34. Staunton, Irene *Mother of the Revolution* (Baobab, Harare, 1990), pp.49 and 81

35. Sweet man, David *African Historical Biographies, Women Leaders in African History*, 1943. Chapter 12, page 97

36. Sylvester, Christine. "Gender" Zimbabwe *The Terrain of Contradictory Development* West View Press, 1992, p.143-152. (65.6023.5y5).

37. United Nations, Fourth World Conference on Women in Beijing

38. "Women in Politics" for National Preparatory Committee—Beijing 1995. 1980

39. *Women, Work, and Gender Relations in Developing Countries*—A Global Perspective. Edited by Parvin Ghorayshi and Claire Belanger. HQ1240 W 6659 1996. p.184.

Figure 1 School Enrollment for Females Still Lags Behind
That for Males in Developing Countries

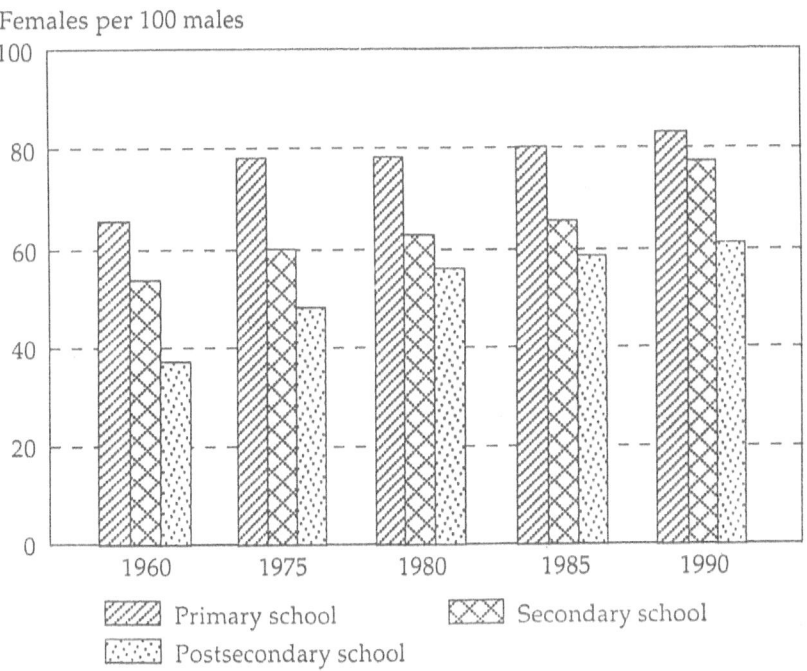

Source: UNESCO Statistical Yearbook 1991.

In postsecondary institutions, as Figure 2 shows, women continue to be overrepresented relative to men in some fields of study: teacher training, the humanities, theology, fine and applied arts, home economics, and

Figure 2 Gender Streaming Excludes Many Women
from Male-Dominated Fields

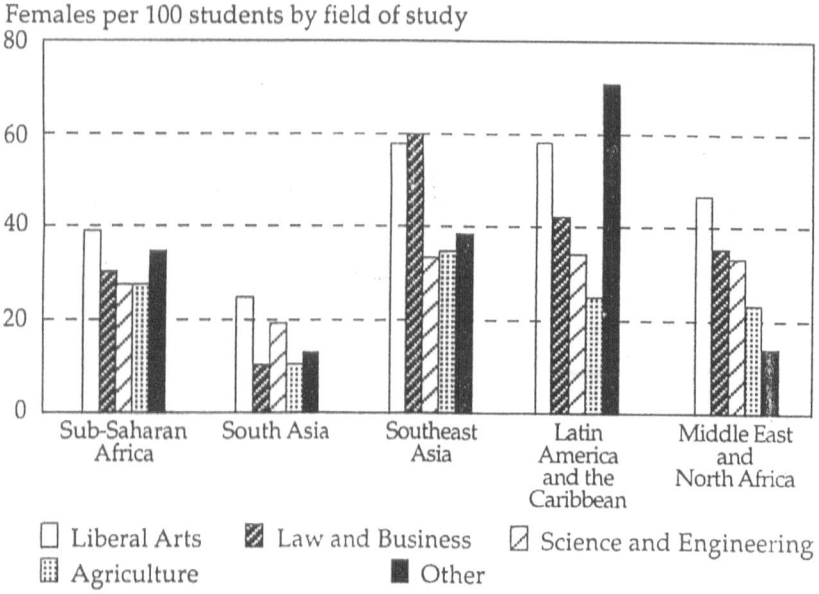

Females per 100 students by field of study

Liberal Arts Law and Business Science and Engineering
Agriculture Other

Source:. United Nations Statistical Office 1990; World Bank staff estimates.